Wounded I Am More Awake

To Dear David

To experience
some of recent
history in Bosnia
as well as
Hope that is
always possible.

Esad Boskalo
P4+. Az,
July 2012

Wounded I Am More Awake

FINDING MEANING AFTER TERROR

Julia Lieblich and Esad Boškailo

Vanderbilt University Press
Nashville

This book is printed on acid-free paper.
Manufactured in the United States of America

Library of Congress Cataloging-in-Publication Data on file

LC control number 2011024786
LC classification DR1313.8 .L54 2012
Dewey class number 949.703

ISBN 978-0-8265-1825-5 (cloth)
ISBN 978-0-8265-1826-2 (paperback)
ISBN 978-0-8265-1827-9 (e-book)

To Mak, Timur, and Aiša Boškailo
and Erica Ramanauskas

They whisper around to me that my life has been in vain
They do not know that so wounded I am more awake.

—Mak Dizdar, "Unwilling Warrior"

Contents

Acknowledgments

We are grateful to the people who had the courage to tell us their stories. In particular, we want to thank Hivzo Šarić, Alija Lizde, Mehmed Dizdar, Huso Obradović, Goran Morić, and the members of the Association of Concentration Camp Survivors of Bosnia-Herzegovina.

Mary Fabri of the Marjorie Kovler Center for survivors of torture has inspired both of us with her commitment to helping patients worldwide heal and find meaning and to teaching the next generation of therapists to become compassionate practitioners. She and her husband, David Goldberg, helped Esad adjust to life in the United States, develop professionally, and regain his trust in humanity.

Nerma Jelačić and Mario Barfus of the International Criminal Tribunal of the Former Yugoslavia provided invaluable assistance, as did the staff of the Court of Bosnia and Herzegovina. We greatly appreciate the work of the Bosnian-Herzegovinian American Academy of Arts and Sciences. We also want to thank the Center for Justice and Accountability, which has successfully used civil laws to hold perpetrators of international human-rights abuses accountable in the United States.

We are indebted to the International Committee of the Red Cross, which sent representatives to see the prisoners in the concentration camps; World Relief Chicago; and the Heartland Alliance for Human Needs and Human Rights.

We couldn't have completed this book without our dear friends Deirdre Stoelzle Graves and Jeff Kelly Lowenstein and the members of the Dart Society, an organization that gives journalists who cover trauma and violence a place of refuge and unwavering support. Deirdre was a generous reader who made invaluable suggestions all along the way. We also want to thank Bruce Shapiro of Columbia University's Dart Center for Journalism and Trauma for his wise counsel.

We are grateful to Stefanie Friedhoff of the Niemen Foundation for Journalism at Harvard University for her commitment to educating journalists about covering trauma and for planning important conferences that have included survivors.

Dean Don Heider and all our colleagues at the Loyola University Chicago School of Communication were an ongoing source of encouragement. A special thanks goes to Loyola's Office of Research Services, which gave us a grant to finish this book, and to Loyola students Molly Aronica and Vivian Mikhail, who assisted with the research.

The leadership of Maricopa County Hospital in Phoenix, including Betsey Bayless, chief executive officer, and Carol Olson, chair of the Department of Psychiatry, strongly supported Esad's work with survivors.

We are indebted to Michael Ames, director of Vanderbilt University Press, for turning a book about trauma into a narrative about meaning, and to Ed Huddleston, managing editor; Sue Havlish, marketing manager; and Jessie Hunnicutt, copy editor, for shepherding this project. We could not have completed the book without the guidance of Sally Arteseros and Meredith Kaffel.

The friends, colleagues, and family members who supported us and shared their reminiscences are too numerous to name. In particular, we would like to express our gratitude to Fondacija Mak Dizdar, Mugdim Karabeg, Ahmed Rahmanović, the Torlo family of Chicago, Dawn Noggle, Colleen Murphy, Sara Laschever, Tim Riley, Arlene Gerson, Nancy Day, Sue Shapiro, Harvey Cox, Marianne Joyce, David Kirkpatrick, Sally Lerman, Brian Connor, Gloria Schmorr, Priscilla Archibald, Christine Stansell, Bernard Golden, and Daniel Rosenthal.

Esad would like to thank his family members: his wife, Aiša; his mother, Emina; and his sister, Biba. Julia would like to thank her father, Malcolm Lieblich. Most of all they are grateful to their children—Esad's sons, Timur and Mak, and Julia's stepdaughter, Erica Ramanauskas—who are continual reminders of the joy that transcends hate.

Part I

CHAPTER 1

The Story of My Life

I was ready to tell
the story of my life
but the ripple of tears
and the agony of my heart
wouldn't let me
      —Rumi, Persian poet (1207–1273)

Hundreds of psychiatrists roamed the hallways of the Toronto hotel. I saw Esad Boškailo and took him for a therapist attending this annual meeting on traumatic stress studies. A tall man with an athletic build, he looked like a doctor on holiday in his loose black sweater and black jeans. But he could also have been a survivor of some terrible trauma who wanted to spend time with therapists who could find Bosnia on a map.

Boškailo chose a session on how journalists cover trauma and took a seat in the third row of the cramped meeting room. I was the lone journalist on the panel, and I was supposed to talk about how reporters should treat their most vulnerable interview subjects. But after a decade of interviewing survivors of trauma in the United States, Latin America, Asia, and Africa, I had given up pretending that a journalist could protect survivors from the aftermath of remembering.

An Afghani woman, I explained to the audience, could not tell me about the death of her son without enduring weeks of headaches. An American tortured in Guatemala had flashbacks of her assailants not long after we talked. An amputee in Sierra Leone spoke of a young man wielding a machete only to have nightmares of the attack.

"Trauma," the amputee told me, "is a special kind of insanity."
And storytelling is a courageous act.

Boškailo listened closely as I spoke, and he approached me as
soon as the session ended. In a thick, central European accent, he
asked me to join him the next day for breakfast.

Over coffee the following morning, I met Boškailo and his
wife, Aiša, a tall, graceful woman with long, dark, curly hair, who
embraced me as if she had known me for years. It turned out that
Boškailo was both a therapist and a survivor: a forty-eight-year-
old psychiatrist, now working in the United States, who more than
ten years after his liberation from Croatian concentration camps
was finally willing to talk about his ordeal.

Boškailo was forceful if only by virtue of his six-foot-two
height and an intensity that let up only when he laughed. A trim
beard framed his olive-skinned face, smooth except for fine lines
around his brown eyes, roundish nose, and full lips. He wore his
dark-brown hair short and spiked, which made him look a little
younger and a lot hipper than most psychiatrists at the conference.

When he finished his espresso, he leaned forward and looked
at me intently, but sat back quickly as if he had thought better of
talking about concentration camps in a café.

Two espressos later, he began again. He had been arrested, he
told me, in his small town in southern Bosnia and taken to the
first of six concentration camps where he spent the better part of
a year. Afterward, he and his family sought refuge in Chicago,
where he began interpreting for and then counseling refugees at
the Bosnian Mental Health Program. Trained in family medicine
in Bosnia, he completed his specialty in psychiatry in Phoenix,
Arizona, where he counseled refugees from many countries with
the International Rescue Committee. Today, he worked with survivors of trauma, from domestic abuse to war.

Would I be interested, he asked, in writing a book about survivors of terror? I was taken aback by this sudden invitation from
a stranger. He had likely read my brief bio in the conference program, but he was clearly more drawn to my approach than to my
credentials. He wanted to talk to someone who understood how
tough it was to talk.

"You understand survivors," he told me. And I gathered he had talked to people who had not.

On the surface, we did not have much in common, except that we were both in our late forties, married, and raising children under twenty. But he was a Muslim man from a small town in Bosnia. And I was a Jewish woman from New York.

Still, the idea was intriguing. As a journalist I had once specialized in writing about religion. Now I found myself drawn to reporting about human rights and people who endured private loss and public trauma. During our brief conversation I suspected that Boškailo had the insight needed to move beyond a tale of atrocities to a meditation on healing. A deeply personal account, I thought, could help both mental health practitioners and survivors of all kinds of loss understand the long-term effects of trauma and the remedies that can help people find meaning after terror.

I could not help thinking of the contribution the Austrian psychiatrist Viktor Frankl had made in his book *Man's Search for Meaning*. Now here was another psychiatrist surviving genocide a half century later and emerging with new insights about how to endure.

As the American psychologist Gordon Allport said of Frankl, "A psychiatrist who personally has faced such extremity is a psychiatrist worth listening to."

So I said yes to the book.

We had big plans for my first trip to Phoenix. Boškailo would come home from the hospital at noon each day, and we would put in a good six hours of work.

I arrived on a Monday at his airy, loftlike ranch house with exposed brick. And I parked my laptop on the dining room table.

On Tuesday, after Boškailo and Aiša headed off to work, I spent my morning hanging out with Boškailo's mother, Emina, a handsome woman wrapped in a wool sweater. We sipped Bosnian coffee as we attempted to communicate with animated hand gestures. Emina talked to me at length in Bosnian, probably in the hope that I might catch a word or two, and I enjoyed the soothing lilt of her voice.

At noon there was no sign of Boškailo. At one o'clock Emina poured me another cup of thick coffee and served me pita, a delicious meat-filled flaky pastry. At three o'clock, Boškailo called to say he had an emergency at work. He walked in the door in time for dinner.

After dinner, we sat at the dining room table, and I started our interview with simple questions.

"How old were you when you arrived at the first camp?"

Boškailo looked perplexed, as if I had asked him about a place he had never been. He was tired, he said. Could we stop for the night and continue the next day?

The next day: More warm conversation with Emina. More coffee and pita. Boškailo walked in just in time for dinner and was too exhausted to talk afterward.

So I got fat on pita while Boškailo continued to put in long workdays.

I suggested that we meet at a coffee shop, but Boškailo insisted on talking at home. He was my host, after all, and he was certain that each evening would be better than the last. But by the final night of my visit, as we sat at the dining room table, he was resigned to the fact that he could not talk about the camps while his wife and children were in the house.

"I'm so sorry," he said.

It was then that I realized his home was his refuge. I was both a guest and an intruder, bringing questions about terror into his sanctuary.

After I left, we found, oddly enough, that we communicated better by phone. Boškailo would sneak into a corner of the house where his family could not hear him and field my endless questions in our stealth interviews.

We spoke most weekday evenings, but there was nothing we enjoyed more than canceling our interviews about torture. Either of us would back out at a moment's notice for the smallest reason—a headache, a work deadline—and the other would never object.

People who work with survivors know the importance of giving them a sense of the control of which they were deprived when they were held captive. So Boškailo chose which topics to discuss, approving or revising my plan for the evening.

He told his story in fragments. It was too painful, he said, to go from beginning to end, something he had never done. He described a moment—a scene, a conversation—and I asked him the questions I needed to write a narrative: Was the wall that surrounded the camps made of bricks? Was there a bathroom? Who emptied the can?

Periodically, he read drafts of my narrative to see if I was capturing the story of his life.

The process for Boškailo was not easy. He could recite the criteria for posttraumatic stress disorder by chapter and verse. The "intrusive memories." The flashbacks. The symptoms that never go away. But after our first interview, he had a panic attack in a small examination room at the hospital where he works, as if he were back in the camps. When I read to him portions of what I had written about his early weeks in captivity, he breathed rapidly and began to cry. Boškailo had been used to maintaining control by doling out his words carefully, telling an anecdote from one camp, offering a quote from another, interrupting a grave account with a joke.

Now he was listening to his story in its entirety, and the nightmares returned.

Sometimes the despair was catching and I would need a break from the project. It usually happened not when we talked about the war, but when Boškailo told me about a man whose life had changed forever in an instant.

Ultimately, Boškailo was certain there would be healing in the telling. And I was convinced there would be healing in the listening. The most profound stories of endurance, I thought, would come from a man who had faced the darkest nights.

CHAPTER 2

Is This Bosnia?

Once upon a time a worthy questioner asked:
Forgive me who is and what sir
Where is
Whence and
Whither sir
Prithee sir
Is this
Bosnia
          —Mak Dizdar, Bosnian poet (1917–1971)

We had worked for a year before Boškailo invited me to Bosnia for a trip that would be more about seeing than talking. He wanted me to imagine his life in Bosnia before the war. We would begin in the south, in his birthplace of Počitelj, an idyllic town built on a rocky cliff on the left bank of the River Neretva. I had seen photographs of Počitelj in decade-old guidebooks, but I was unprepared for this seemingly untouched Ottoman enclave surrounded by a ten-foot-high stone wall.

In the center of the old town stood the Mosque of Šišman Ibrahim-Paša, one of Bosnia's finest in the classical Ottoman style. The mosque, I would learn, lost its dome and minaret when Croats set off an explosion in 1993 to terrorize the Bosnian Muslim community, though at the time there was no military action in Počitelj. The building had since been restored to its original splendor.

A fifteenth-century silo-shaped fort overlooked rows of white-washed stone houses built into the steep hills. Just two decades earlier, Boškailo told me, about a thousand Bosnian Muslims and

Croats lived on these hills, and busloads of panting tourists visited, walking up the slippery rock paths to see the mosque, the tower, and the paintings displayed by artists attending Počitelj's international art colony.

Now on a hot July morning, Boškailo and I were the only ones stopping at the outdoor gift shop with its undisturbed rows of copper coffeepots. And I was the lone visitor looking at landscapes in the art colony's gallery.

We sat down for coffee in a café bar surrounded by gardens in the center of town. It looked like a tourist restaurant in the off season with its empty tables and bored waiters smoking cigarettes. But Boškailo asked me to picture a different place, a café teaming with life every morning and evening.

In his jeans and black T-shirt, he was more relaxed than I had seen him in the States, as if all that espresso had a calming effect. And he was determined that I keep refilling my small cup with coffee, if only so that I could better imagine.

Every night, he said, dozens of his friends came down from the hills and crowded into the café bar or sat on the patio shaded by grape leaves, listening to Donna Summer.

From the time he was fourteen he would meet his friends at the café bar each night and stay until he had downed his seventh espresso. It was about the coffee, he said languidly, and also not about the coffee. It was more about being completely relaxed while they talked about work, philosophy, and cars.

"We have a word for it in Bosnian," he said. "*Ćeif*. Extreme pleasure. The beauty of enjoying something on the highest level."

He was in his twenties in the mid-1980s. He had already graduated from the Sarajevo University Medical School, and he was working an 8 a.m. to 1:30 p.m. shift in family medicine in a community hospital and living in his parents' home. He was not a psychiatrist yet. His only experience was a psychiatric rotation in the hospital.

"But I knew our coffee meetings were a kind of psychotherapy," he said, smiling. "If you had a problem at work, you could talk to a friend for five or six hours. No one told you when your time was up."

He had good friends in Počitelj, the kind that were supposed to last a lifetime given that no one was expected to leave home for more than a year or two.

There was Kapa, his best friend. Like Boškailo, Kapa was a solid man with a strong chin. But Boškailo had a wild mane of curly black hair while Kapa's was straight and blond.

Boškailo never liked to plan his next move. Kapa, a mechanical technician, always had a project. He could weld, fix motors, and assemble anything. While Boškailo played soccer, Kapa made radios. He designed the first remote-control garage door in Počitelj after he saw it in a movie, and he built a fireplace when nobody had a fireplace.

"What drew you to Kapa?" I asked Boškailo.

"He was gentle, very gentle. He was my brother and I could depend on him: to give me a ride, fix my car, or just sit with me for hours. He was a good listener, maybe because he never talked much.

"I once asked Kapa why he never talked. He said the rest of us talked nonsense, so why should he join in."

Another close friend of Boškailo's was a dentist. The dentist—as Boškailo called him—was a handsome, dark-skinned man with a chiseled face. He always wore jeans, sneakers, and a white T-shirt that set off his muscular physique.

The dentist was as unpredictable as Kapa was solid. He was the kind of guy who would speed through a school zone and brake in a war zone. During a conversation, he would challenge everyone in the room.

"If I said a soccer team was good, he would say the team was bad," Boškailo said. "He provoked arguments, and he enjoyed seeing people argue."

"Did you like the dentist?" I asked.

"I often wondered what I saw in him. But there was another side to him. He never charged poor people for dental care. He didn't tell them he wouldn't charge them. At the end he'd say, 'That's okay.' Thousands of dollars' worth of medical care, and he'd give it all away."

The friends met every night after work and drove to café bars in nearby towns. They could count on seeing the regulars at their tables, like Boškailo's former chemistry professor, Hivzo, a short, chubby guy only a few years older than Boškailo who looked more like a Swede than a Bosnian with his pale, round face and blond hair.

"When we were in school he would try to be tough with us, but he couldn't because he was too nice. We couldn't imagine him angry. He was optimistic to the point of being naive, and I would need that optimism."

The professor was always with his best friend, Professor Djevenica, who at six-foot-six towered over him as they played cards and sipped their drinks. Djevenica looked intimidating at first glance, Boškailo said, but he was a good guy who was always in a good mood.

Hivzo was Bosnian Muslim and Djevenica was Croatian Catholic. "But to me, they were just the professor and the professor, like an old married couple," Boškailo said. "Even during the break at school they would join each other for coffee."

Boškailo and Aiša had dated in the café bars. They had been introduced while Boškailo was in medical school and she was studying laboratory science at a nursing college, and had met for coffee every three or four months. Then they did not see each other for two years until one day he spotted her on the street and stopped her.

"I was a doctor and she was working in a microbiology lab in Mostar, twenty minutes north of my town. She was just beautiful for me. Oh my God," he said, a youthful flush returning to his face. "She had long, curly black hair and was tall and thin. As long as I had known her, she had never complained about small things. She took a stand when it mattered.

"I wanted to spend every minute with her. From then on, every afternoon we went to the Adriatic Sea to swim. We went to a restaurant with music where we joked and sang *sevdah*, songs about lost love. And then we went to the café bar to be with my friends."

Two weeks after he stopped her on the street, he asked her to marry him, and they invited a Bosnian imam to come to Boškailo's house the next day to perform the ceremony in his living room. They were not traditionally religious. Although the country was more than 40 percent Muslim, during Communist rule few people were observant. Later they had a wedding party on the Croatian coast.

"My best man, Boro, was Serbian, but I only mention that now. He had been my roommate in medical school for five years and was among my closest friends."

The couple moved into Boškailo's parents' house in the summer of 1988, and one year later their son Timur was born, followed by Mak. Kapa, Boškailo's best friend, had married a Croatian woman named Vera, and the four of them spent long evenings together in the café bars.

Some Bosnians said they saw a change coming in the spring of 1990. Kapa saw it coming. But Boškailo reveled in his belief in goodwill among friends.

"I knew nothing," he said, leaning back in his chair. Sipping espresso in the café bar back then with his wife and friends, he had pictured peaceful days slipping into years. And he had marveled at his own good luck.

CHAPTER 3
The Night Is So Unreal

The night is so unreal—
And far too quiet. And there is no one
To tell us: Tomorrow, for you—horror.
Tomorrow, for you—love.
                    —Abdulah Sidran, Bosnian poet (1944–)

The Croats did not know the first thing about running a concentration camp. Roses lined the stone wall surrounding the
former army training school in Čapljina, a small town near
Počitelj. And the three middle-aged guards at the gate looked
more ready for sleeping than for fighting in a war that had yet
to begin.

A scrawny-looking guard escorted a handful of men down
the road to a two-story dormitory on the manicured grounds.
Boškailo was in his early thirties then, six-foot-two and 220 pounds.
He could easily have overtaken the guard. But he followed, if only
to see what would happen next.

"Esad!" he heard from the back of a large, smoky room on the
first floor of the building. Everyone was there, thirty or so people
sitting on military cots with cigarettes in their hands. Boškailo
saw his dentist friend, wearing jeans and a T-shirt that showed off
his muscles, and the professor, Hivzo, looking like a lost Swede
among Bosnians.

A dozen men surrounded Boškailo, taking turns kissing him
on each cheek, as if they had not just seen him in the café bars a
few days earlier.

The professor asked him to sit on a cot near his, and the dentist
handed him a cigarette and a bottle of whiskey.

"What are we doing here?" Boškailo asked. "And when are we getting out?"

"Soon," the professor assured him. "I have a Croatian friend who's now in the defense ministry."

That would be Professor Djevenica, his old pal from the café bar. "Djevenica is not going to get you out," Boškailo thought. "He's the one who put you in."

The two guards sitting in the front of the room seemed a little sheepish watching over a dormitory of familiar faces. Who wanted to lock up the professor who had taught him in high school or the doctor who had stitched his wounds?

Boškailo recognized one of the guards, Boko, a short, chubby man in his late forties with a military haircut. He recognized Boškailo, too.

"You're the doctor," he said, as if Boškailo might be handy to have around. He used to be a waiter in a café bar, and he struck Boškailo as too dull to be dangerous.

Soon Boškailo was sitting on the floor with cards in one hand and a bottle in the other. The professor went on about how they would be released at any moment. The dentist told him he was dreaming. Boškailo had a hard enough time comprehending that he could not just walk out the door and head home; he could not think about whether they would be held for days or weeks. Not until three o'clock in the morning was he drunk enough to sleep.

They were awakened early by the guards bringing a pot of slop for breakfast, but they took their time finishing their coffee in tin cups. At nine, the guards called out work assignments, odd jobs around the grounds like picking up trash and pulling weeds, but their orders sounded more like suggestions. Outside, Boškailo walked slowly up and down the grassy fields, partly out of rebellion, partly to make the hours pass. And none of the guards objected when the men took long breaks sitting on the grass and enjoying a cigarette.

Five to ten more men arrived each day, convinced they would be released shortly. Friends who had heard they had been arrested stopped by throughout the day to bring them food and whiskey.

One afternoon a dozen men from Počitelj carrying a roasted ox came to see Boškailo.

"Esad, would you like us to pray here?"

"No, it's too dirty here for our prayers," he said.

Later, a guard carrying a shotgun told Boškailo to tell the crowd to leave.

"You do it," Boškailo told him. "You are the guard, not me."

———

Aiša visited two days later, and they tried to keep the conversation light with news of four-year-old Timur and two-year-old Mak. But when they had a moment of privacy, he urged her to leave the country immediately.

"Pack up the kids and go to Italy."

But Aiša refused to leave him behind.

Her face was all he needed to remind him of the seriousness of the situation, which sometimes seemed more comical than dire. By her third visit she looked worse than he did. She was delicate with large brown eyes and brown hair. Now she looked gaunt and frightened. She wasn't eating, and she was running around trying in vain to find someone—at the hospital, at the Democratic Party headquarters—who could get him out.

Kapa visited every other day. He brought cigarettes and food and the promise that someone besides Aiša was looking out for him.

Kapa was not much of a talker, but months before the war with the Croats, when nobody thought there would be a war, he said they were going to fight for their lives.

CHAPTER 4

How Can This Happen Here?

The old man on the bridge, who whispers . . .
How can this happen
Here, of all places, where we're so humane?
        —Semezdin Mehmedinović, Bosnian poet (1960–)

Did Bosnian Muslims—known as Bosniaks—Croat Catholics, and Serbian Orthodox Christians really get along before the fighting that led to the first concentration camps in Europe since World War II?

"If you put ten Bosnians in a room today and ask them that question, half will say we got along famously and the other half will say we never got along," Boškailo told me. "Both are right."

The historian Sabrina Ramet, who analyzed more than 130 books on Yugoslavia in four languages, found "a dizzying array of competing interpretations." Scholars still debate such topics as how large a role religion played in the war, whether the Serbs were guilty of genocide, and whether Western nations should have intervened earlier in the war—or not at all.

Boškailo rejects theories that Serbs, Croats, and Bosniaks were "ancient enemies" somehow predisposed to violence. He agrees with the historian Noel Malcolm, who says that beginning in the late 1800s religious and ethnic communities lived peacefully for more than one hundred years, except during and just after World War I and during World War II. In 1914, a young Serbian nationalist shot and killed Archduke Franz Ferdinand, heir to the Hapsburg throne, and his wife, Sofia, on the streets of Sarajevo. The assassination precipitated the start of World War I.

Nazi Germany invaded Yugoslavia in 1941, and a fascist

government was installed under the Croatian politician Ante Pavelić. With the help of Hitler and Mussolini, Pavelić organized the Ustasha movement for Croatian independence. During the war, the Ustasha executed between seventy thousand and one hundred thousand Serbs, Jews, and Gypsies at Jasenovac, a concentration camp in Croatia. In February 1943, local Serb forces slaughtered more than nine thousand Bosniaks in Bosnia's Foča-Čajniče region.

The Germans began to withdraw from Yugoslavia in the summer of 1944, and Allied powers persuaded King Peter of Yugoslavia to appeal to his country to back the Communist leader Josip Broz Tito, who had started an antifascist organization to resist the Germans. Tito liberated the region from the Germans and formed the Socialist Federal Republic of Yugoslavia with Slovenia, Croatia, Bosnia, Montenegro, Macedonia, and Serbia, and the two autonomous provinces of Kosovo and Vojvodina. Tito's early years were brutal. According to Malcolm, up to 250,000 people were killed in mass shootings, concentration camps, and death marches between 1945 and 1946. But by the 1960s, Tito began to liberalize his policies, heralding a new era often described as idyllic.

"The new attitude under Tito was, Let's live together as if nothing had happened," Boškailo said. "Every single day the TV talked about unity and brotherhood among the Serbs, Croats, and Bosniaks. We were ordered to get along, and we did." In the 1980s, 30 percent of marriages were "mixed," he notes. "And Bosniaks, Croats, and Serbs lived together like family. These *were* good times. We had no idea that underneath our friendship was a simmering nationalism."

———

Boškailo was only twenty-one in 1980 when Tito died and communism began to fall apart. His parents talked endlessly about how the six Yugoslav republics were vying for power as the economy collapsed. They lamented the rise of nationalism in Serbia and the growing alliance between nationalistic political leaders and the press, but Boškailo did not pay much attention to the talking heads on the TV news.

That was until 1986, when Serbia's forty-four-year-old Communist Party leader and former banker, Slobodan Milošević, came to power. By then Boškailo was twenty-seven, and he was struck by Milošević's cool demeanor and the way he slicked his thick gray hair back like James Dean. "When a Serbian journalist friend told me, 'This guy is really scary,' I was not ready to agree. 'What do you really know about him?' I asked. I even felt a little sorry for the guy, Milošević. Everyone knew that both his parents had killed themselves, and I could not imagine such a fate."

Milošević started out organizing meetings with hundreds of people, and it was not long before he was drawing crowds of more than a million with promises of a "Greater Serbia" and an end to years of Serb victimization. He was always on television, and his message was always the same: Serbs were in danger because the Croats, Bosniaks, Slovenians, and Albanians wanted to kill them. Milošević's goal, he said, was to protect the Serbs, and he had the means: he controlled the well-equipped Yugoslav army.

By the time Boškailo married Aiša in 1988, he considered Milošević a crazy fanatic, but he still doubted that the man had any real influence over Bosnian Serbs. Besides, war was unthinkable. How could Bosnian Serbs form a front line in a country where Serbs, Croats, and Bosniaks lived as neighbors? His best man was Serbian. His schoolmates were Croatian. Did Milošević really expect Serbians to turn on their friends?

Moreover, few Bosnians believed that the United Nations and the United States would let such a thing happen in Europe in the 1990s.

Boškailo's chemistry professor, Hivzo, caught in the euphoria over the collapse of communism, became active in the Bosnian Democratic Party. Boškailo's uncle, Bećir, the regional director of the party, blamed communism for the lack of freedom of speech and religion and wanted more than anything to see its demise. Handsome and fit with long gray hair and an unusually warm and effusive manner, he almost cried when he asked Boškailo to join the Democratic Party.

"He was like a second father to me," Boškailo said, "and I hated to say no to him. But I did not think doctors should be joining political parties."

When Boškailo lost his own father after a six-month illness, Bećir became more than a second father. Not a day passed when he didn't stop by the Boškailo home to offer his prayers and assistance. While many Bosnian men expressed little affection in public and would not be caught dead hugging, Bećir wrapped his family in his arms.

In the summer of 1991, Serbia attacked Croatia. Boškailo believed that the violence should be attributed not to religious differences, but to the Serb leadership's political strategy and a failed Western policy that rejected air strikes and supported an arms embargo that left Bosniaks and Croats defenseless against the well-armed Serbs.

But those states had a long-standing history of conflict, and neither Bećir nor Boškailo thought Bosnia would be next.

Then on April 6, 1992, the international community recognized Bosnia as an independent state, and Serbia attacked Bosnia.

Radovan Karadžić, a former psychiatrist from Montenegro who practiced in Sarajevo, commanded a renegade Serbian army in Bosnia with Milošević's support. Boškailo knew of Karadžić as a doctor who worked at a hospital associated with his medical school. He had been a disheveled man with long, scraggly hair. Now he was heading an army.

Under Karadžić's leadership, Bosnian Serb nationalists and the Yugoslav army began a policy of "ethnic cleansing" to establish a "pure" Serb republic, using direct shelling and sniper attacks to force Bosniaks and Croats out of key sections of Bosnia. When people said that the Serbs were running a concentration camp in Serbian-held Bosnian territory, Boškailo heard echoes of World War II.

The result was the first genocide in Europe since World War II. Milošević wanted to create a Greater Serbia encompassing all lands where Serbs lived, and his paramilitary began to systematically terrorize and kill non-Serbs in Bosnia.

The United Nations sent peacekeepers to Sarajevo in the

summer of 1992. But Serb gunners attacked the convoys, preventing the distribution of aid to Bosnians who needed it most.

In August 1992, the world learned the full extent of the atrocities when journalists reported the mass rapes of women and the slaughter of prisoners in concentration camps. The *Newsday* correspondent Roy Gutman wrote on August 2, "The Serb conquerors of northern Bosnia have established two concentration camps in which more than a thousand civilians have been executed or starved and thousands more are being held until they die." During the war, the Serbs would run dozens of such camps in northern Bosnia, and later the Croats would operate concentration camps in the south.

The Bosnian government, the police, the Bosnian army, and the Croatian Defense Council (HVO) quickly formed an army. It was a natural alliance. There was never a question that Bosniaks and Croats should be together. The Serbs were attacking the country.

When the battle broke out, Boškailo sent his family to a small town on the Croatian coast, and he joined the Bosnian and Croatian forces fighting the Serbs as an army medical doctor. He spent his waking hours setting up infirmaries near the front line less than a mile from his home.

During the first two weeks, he established an infirmary in Domanovići, a small town two miles northeast of Počitelj with two doctors (one Croatian and one Bosniak) and six nurses (three Croatian and three Bosniak) in an abandoned office in the basement of an apartment building. He had been trained to be an army medical officer in the Yugoslav army, but now they had few weapons and fewer instructions. They just knew that the Serbs were coming from the east.

"When the fighting started I was never more scared in my life. We would hear the sound of an explosion and we had no idea how close it was.

"Wounded soldiers began arriving by the dozen. We got people with small cars to drive the injured to hospitals, some with their legs hanging over the back. Soon grenades were exploding all around us.

"Maybe it would have been easier if I had not known so many of the men. A Croatian neighbor of mine brought in another neighbor, Martin, who played soccer with me. He was wounded on the left side of his chest and bleeding badly, and he was screaming in pain. I stopped his bleeding. I put in an IV line in him. But he knew he was dying. I saw it in his eyes. He said, 'Take care of my kids.' I sent him to the hospital in a car, and he died a half hour later."

The same day at 4 or 5 p.m. the shooting stopped completely. No grenades. No explosions. The soldiers nearby told Boškailo it looked like the fighting had ceased.

That night he sat outside having coffee with a Croatian doctor. "She was the best doctor in the community, and with her I felt safe. She was a very tall woman, probably six-foot-two or three, and a little older than I was. I had some kind of crazy optimism about the war being over. But she said, 'It's not going to be okay, Esad. There is going to be a bloodbath.'"

A few days later he returned to Počitelj, where thousands of refugees, mostly Croatian, had already flooded the town. They were staying in cars and houses. Sixty Croats were sleeping in his empty house. He was never there—he was at the front line and his family was on the Croatian Coast—so he offered them the key and told them to eat whatever food they could find.

"People came up to me and touched me, surprised I was alive. Everyone thought our medical unit had been wiped out. I saw Martin's father, and he asked me if I had seen his son. I lied to his father. I said I had not seen Martin. In the first days of the war I could not tell a father he had lost his son."

Boškailo set up an infirmary in his town with beds in an old school built during the time of the Ottoman Empire. By 9 a.m. he had six soldiers. His goal was to send the wounded to a hospital in Čapljina on the west side of the River Neretva.

His best friend, Kapa, worked in a building next to the infirmary, and Boškailo felt better just having him around. Kapa was a full-time commander and was resettling Croatian and Bosniak refugees, whose numbers grew from one thousand to ten thousand in less than a week. Kapa stayed calm as he organized the distribution of food, water, milk, and cigarettes. And he kept Boškailo calm as the bodies kept coming.

Boškailo's uncle Bećir volunteered to help Kapa, and the two became a team: the stoic Kapa and the emotive Bećir, both committed to efficiency in a crisis.

Bećir coordinated food distribution. He went to a large local market and gathered as much food as he could fit into a truck. Then he went from door to door with his two teenage daughters asking parents and children, most of whom were Croatian, if they needed rations. He was already in his fifties, but he got by on little sleep.

"Slow down, Uncle," Boškailo pleaded when he saw him.

"Yes, I need to get rest," he responded. But he did not rest. Boškailo called his uncle a *melek*—an angel. He was a religious man, though he rarely talked about it. Bećir would go to a corner to say his five daily prayers.

Kapa, meanwhile, had the foresight to pick up paintings housed at the art colony and take them for protection to an abandoned prison from the Ottoman period that few people knew existed. He carried Yugoslav's treasures—paintings by Sefet Zec, Halil Tikveša, and Affan Ramić—and he built a solid door for the prison with a strong lock.

When they heard the Serbian soldiers approaching, Kapa knew they had to get all the refugees to Čapljina. But the Serbs would not let them pass by land. So Kapa came up with a crazy idea: they would go by boat.

He went around town asking local people to volunteer their small boats. And he asked the refugees, many of whom could not swim, to crowd into vessels meant to hold only four or five people for the five-minute ride across one hundred yards of deep river. Working around the clock, Kapa sent thousands of people across the River Neretva, and no one was killed along the way.

Boškailo and Kapa, along with Kapa's cousin Mirza, who looked fifteen but was old enough to fight, and two others, stayed behind in a house across from the art colony. When they saw the Serbs coming closer, they got into a small boat and let the strong current of the river carry them. But Mirza wanted to go back to care for his ailing mother. So he jumped out and swam to shore. "They will kill you," Boškailo shouted. "They will kill you." But Mirza did not listen. The remaining four men made it across the river and hiked to Medjugorje, the famed holy site where Catholics saw apparitions of Mary, the Mother of Peace.

That's where they learned that the Serbs had shot and killed Mirza.

In the summer of 1992, Boškailo set up their next infirmary on the Čapljina front line while soldiers and civilians made plans to recapture Počitelj from the Serbs. An old friend, Cakan, had moved from Bosnia to Croatia at age eighteen to marry a Croatian woman. Now he had come back to run a training camp for Bosniak soldiers in Medjugorje.

Cakan had few soldiers to work with, seventy good ones at most, but they were joining Croats with heavy artillery already positioned on the west bank of the River Neretva. Cakan trained his men well, and he was determined to take back his town.

In the evenings, and sometimes during the day, Kapa, dressed as a civilian, walked around territory held by the Serbs recording military positions.

At 6 p.m. on June 5, Cakan led his group of seventy, along with Kapa and Boškailo carrying packs of medical supplies, to the river. They waited there until 10 p.m.

Then, in small boats, they crossed the river and staked out their positions above Počitelj.

Boškailo, another doctor, and two technicians ran to the nearby house of a friend to set up an infirmary in the basement. There was no electricity in the garage so they used lighters. They set up an operating area on a table tennis board.

At 5 a.m., their Croatian allies started firing with heavy artillery, and Cakan ordered his men to shoot. Boškailo had never heard such a thundering noise.

Six bodies arrived at his infirmary the first day, all neighbors, all dead. The wounded came quickly, and Boškailo and his team removed bullets, applied compresses, and stitched wounds. When his cousin came in with wounds in his abdomen, arms, and legs, they sent him by boat to a surgeon in a better-equipped medical unit in a tunnel on the west bank of the River Neretva, and they organized a transport system for the most severely injured.

Boškailo and his team saved every soldier who arrived still breathing.

As Cakan's troops advanced on Day Three so did Boškailo, who headed to an old school to open a new infirmary. He and a commander rode along the tree-lined street from Počitelj to Sto-lac, a route Boškailo had driven a thousand times. All around him he saw burning houses and burning bodies. Men were slumped over cars and lying in the street. He had never seen anything like it. Never.

Cakan and his men kept advancing, and the Serbs gradually retreated.

In just three days, Cakan and his band of soldiers retook Počitelj and Stolac. It was the longest three days of Boškailo's life.

———

A lanky man in his early twenties arrived at Boškailo's infirmary crying in pain. "What's your name?" Boškailo asked. The man just shook with fever and did not answer.

Boškailo put an IV in him and stopped the bleeding in his chest and shoulder, but he wanted to send him to the better-equipped medical unit.

"I'm in pain," the man said.

Boškailo was surprised, then, when the man began walking around with his IV to help take care of the other patients. He applied compresses on one man's wound with the skill of a professional.

"Are you a doctor?" Boškailo asked.

"No," he said.

"Are you from this area?"

"I am from Vukovar." Vukovar was a large city in Croatia that was destroyed during the Serbian-Croatian war. Because there were few doctors, the man said, everyone had to learn first aid.

Several minutes later, Boškailo's colleague looked up from his work and noticed the young man.

"Look at his uniform. He is a Chetnik," his colleague shouted. "He's a Chetnik!" A Chetnik was a Serb. Boškailo had been so busy with the wounds he had not noticed the uniform.

The colleague took off his gloves and took the man's wallet from his pants.

"Saša Zurovac!"

His name was well known. His picture had been in all the newspapers when he was accused of murdering an elderly Bosniak couple in a Mostar market. He had scrawled his name in blood on the wall of a building.

"I worked in a kitchen!" Zurovac protested. "I've never been a soldier."

As word got out that they had Zurovac, an angry mob of thirty armed people, including children, gathered outside. Boškailo grabbed his big gun and went to meet them.

"This is my infirmary. This is a wounded soldier, and he is going to stay alive." They backed down, and he put Zurovac in an ambulance with a Bosnian driver.

"He arrived alive, and that is all I cared about. I figured that he would probably be tried and killed later. I really did not care. My job was done."

Through the rest of 1992, Boškailo oversaw three infirmaries at the front line next to command central, working first out of houses off the road between Počitelj and Stolac and later in homes between Stolac and Mostar. When the violence subsided in Počitelj, Aiša and the children returned home, and Boškailo was able to join them every few weeks for a day or two.

During periods of relative calm, his infirmaries functioned more like emergency rooms. He treated children and adults with injuries and acute and chronic illnesses. After seeing dozens of civilians in an afternoon, he almost forgot that Bosnia was at war. Then one afternoon outside the first infirmary, a soldier carrying a Croatian flag walked up to the house, dug into the dirt with the end of the stick, and pushed the Croatian flag into the ground.

Boškailo came outside as the Croat stood back and admired his work.

"This is Bosnia," Boškailo said.

"This is Croatia," the soldier said. If Boškailo moved the flag, the Croat said, he would have to shoot.

Boškailo had a hard time taking seriously this sudden bout of nationalism from a Croat. But in the upcoming months, tensions between Bosnians and Croats heightened.

Without explanation, Croatian leaders declared Croatian the official language of Bosnia, and students were forbidden to speak the Bosnian language in school, though there were only small differences in the languages, given that they had the same roots. Croatian school administrators and business leaders began to fire Bosniaks from their jobs as government workers, teachers, and judges.

Boškailo had heard that in Croatian churches throughout the region, priests had polled parishioners on whether they were in favor of cleansing the area of Bosniaks. At first most of the parishioners were against ethnic cleansing. When a third vote was held weeks later, almost everyone was for it.

"I felt a little guilty about having trusted the Croats," Boškailo told me. "Why had I not listened to neighbors who said that the Croats had sided with the fascists during World War II and would turn on us again? My wife, Aiša, had not been as trusting. She had seen the change in the Croatian children first when they began playing games tagging Muslim children as the enemies.

"For me, the feelings of betrayal did not come from the fact that we had been neighbors. We had joined together to defend ourselves against the Serbs. We had risked our lives. But we had been an army of convenience, so perhaps the camaraderie never ran deep."

———

Boškailo had suspected that the Croatian secret police would come for him. They had already arrested some Bosniak politicians, doctors, lawyers, and professors, anyone with any influence. It was a good way to instill fear in the rest of the people.

Animosity between Croats and Bosniaks only increased. Mate Boban, the Croatian leader, and Radovan Karadžić, the Serb leader, had already met several times at the end of 1992 and the beginning of 1993 to decide how to divide up Bosnia. Then Boškailo heard stories that the Croats had taken over other towns. Croatian leaders in Čapljina had assured the local Bosniaks that everything was fine, but Bosniaks heard that behind the scenes they were strategizing about a separation.

Local Bosniak leaders asked Boškailo and five others to go to Germany to try to raise money from their supporters and gather food and clothing needed during the war with Serbia. The six men stayed overnight at a hotel in Zagreb, Croatia. In the lobby, Boškailo spotted the head of the regional secret police standing with several officers by the reception desk. He recognized most of the men. If he had met them two weeks earlier, they would likely have jumped up to greet him at such a chance meeting. Today they carried rifles instead of their usual handguns and their blank expressions gave him chills.

When the officers saw Boškailo and his friends, the six Bosniaks ran out of the lobby and raced up the steps to their hotel room. Boškailo received a telephone call from his sister, who told him that Croatian soldiers were arresting Bosniak leaders in Čapljina. The group decided that three men would continue on to Germany to complete their mission and the rest would return home to handle the crisis. Boškailo and two others jumped through the second-floor window and caught the next bus to Bosnia.

They rode through Croatia and continued south to Počitelj. A passenger was raging to no one in particular about how Bosniaks were ruining the country. Perhaps he was drunk, Boškailo thought. The television and newspapers were full of such talk, but it was the first time he had heard anyone proclaim anti-Bosniak propaganda so openly so close to his home.

That night his cousin came over and said he had heard there were going to be more arrests in Počitelj. If Boškailo ran away, he told him, they would go after his family.

The next morning—April 20, 1993—Boškailo told Aiša that the police were coming and he did not want their two sons to see them arrest him. She started to cry, but they went to a café bar and waited.

He asked her to go to a safe place—Mostar, twenty miles away— for a short stay. He told her not to worry, he would be back soon. He had some kind of crazy hope. Maybe they would not arrest him.

As they drank their espressos, they saw a unit of two dozen Croatian soldiers lined up as if waiting for someone. Two of them—young men in their early twenties—approached Boškailo. They had guns hanging on their belts. One man pressed a gun to Boškailo's head and asked him to come with them.

"It was not like a war we had seen on television," Boškailo recalled. "People all around us were sitting in the café bar, walking on the street, shopping for food. Now they were standing in place, staring at us.

"The two soldiers looked as scared as I was. They were shaking a little. When I asked them if they had a warrant, they just shrugged. They didn't cuff me. They asked me to please get into their car. I kissed my wife and followed them."

When they arrived in Čapljina, the solders told Boškailo to bow down in the back seat. "Doctor, you know it's not going to be nice if the people see you've been arrested."

"I don't know how to bow down," he said.

CHAPTER 5

The Thin Air of Hope

Prisoners still breathe the thin air
Of hope
As a cold dew
Falls on their bare
Feet
—Mak Dizdar

Now Boškailo was smoking in a barracks run by Croatian guards and thinking he could imagine worse punishments than drinking with his friends. They were an odd group, the dozen Bosniaks who ate together, played cards together, and slept in the same corner. He guessed that was the prison mentality: trust only your own.

The professor, Hivzo, remained oddly optimistic, as if nothing truly bad could happen. Nothing seemed to shake that confidence, Boškailo thought, not even Hivzo's best friend's betrayal.

The dentist remained belligerent, providing a running commentary on camp life regardless of who was listening. Boškailo worried he would lose his temper or try to provoke Boko, the guard.

Goran, a journalist, had a Croatian mother, which gave them an in with the guards. He was good-looking, in his late thirties with long blond hair. He had been a factory worker before he quit his job to form a political magazine about the new democracy movement. In Bosnia, they give people nicknames that are the opposite of their personalities. Goran was "Nerves" because of his unnerving calm.

Then there was Sejo, who tended to meld into any crowd. He was an average businessman in his midthirties. He had a peaceful nature.

Days turned into weeks. But as long as local politicians were still talking of negotiation, life at the camp remained fairly relaxed. The men played cards for hours and sang sevdah. They did not have an accordion, but they imagined one. Somebody would start singing slowly, one song and then another. They all knew the words and could sing the same songs over and over again:

> Oh the strange suffering from the city of Mostar
> Since last year, until right now
> How Biba suffers from a broken heart
> Čelebić Biba suffers from heartbreak
> Suffers, but tells no one
> Suffers, but tells no one

When they stopped singing aloud, the men hummed.

Mostly they spent time just sitting and not saying a word. What did they have to say when there was no news? Boškailo knew Goran was thinking about his wife. Goran knew he was thinking about Aiša.

The guards, except for Boko, left them alone. Boko would tell them to stop singing when it got on his nerves. The worst was when Boko would hold court with incoherent rants about how Bosnia should be given to the state of Croatia. He singled out Boškailo to listen to his ailments, and Boškailo would taunt him. Boko would tell the doctor he was dizzy, and Boškailo would look into his eyes and say, "Boko, you have ten days to live."

The dentist was less patient. He would curse at the guards and call them fascists.

"You are the biggest fascist of all," he would tell Boko, who seemed impervious to the dentist's insults. In 1941, Germans and Italians had invaded the Balkans, and Croatia had set up a fascist government sympathetic to the Nazis. But no guard wanted to be reminded of such a past.

The guards still had no clue what to do with their prisoners, and the prisoners did not know how to think about being held in this place. No one was being tortured. No one had been shot.

Conditions on the inside reflected life on the outside. When the radio broadcasts reported a possible peace agreement, the guards would open the doors, buy the men cigarettes, and bring them food from home. One night a guard brought them fifty cucumbers—a goodwill gesture in case they were released.

But when a leader of the Croatian Democratic Union, a nationalist party, said on television that Croats should kill all Bosniaks, it was no longer safe for Bosniaks to walk in Čapljina. Soon more Bosniak men were being brought to the camp each day, until fifty people were sleeping on the cold cement floor of the barracks next to the lucky men on the cots.

Then on May 15, 1993, war broke out between the Croats and the Bosniaks. That was when Boko locked the doors to the barracks and turned Aiša away at the gate.

One guard, Dadić, was a reasonable guy, and he urged Boškailo not to antagonize Boko. Boko was a madman, Dadić told him, but Boškailo could not take the warning seriously.

It was Dadić who arranged one more visit with Boškailo's family. Boškailo had to see them because he had to tell them to run away. He did not tell anyone they were coming, and he could not quite believe it early one morning when he saw Aiša, two-year-old Mak, four-year-old Timur, his mother, and his uncle walking toward him as he stood in front of the barracks. His sons broke into a run and jumped into his arms, and soon he was hugging all of them tightly.

Two minutes after they arrived, he saw Boko coming toward them with a gun.

"Who gave you permission?" he shouted at Aiša. "Leave now or I'll shoot you."

Boškailo said goodbye quickly, but Mak grabbed onto his father's shirt with his small hands and wouldn't let go. His mother pulled him, but Mak held onto his father with both arms and legs.

"Daddy, Daddy, Daddy," he screamed. "Daddy, Daddy, Daddy."

Boko pushed the boy away and shoved Boškailo into the barracks. All around him he saw men crying for their children.

Boko had found a new purpose with the new war. Beefier than ever, the dull café waiter was finally a real guard with a real concentration camp. Boškailo thought Boko could smell the prisoners' fear and it gave him a feeling of increasing power. And new prisoners like Benca, Aiša's former literature professor, would feel his wrath most.

Benca was more influential than the rest of the prisoners. He had been the president of the Communist Party in his community and later the mayor of the Bosnian town of Stolac. Boškailo caught a glimpse of Benca when he and four others arrived at the dormitory before they were taken to the freezing-cold basement.

On the first night the dentist held Boškailo while he climbed up onto the high window ledge and opened the window with a stick. He dropped cigarettes into Benca's cell and shivered when he heard his screams.

When the five men were brought upstairs ten days later, Boškailo saw the dried blood and welts on Benca's face.

Boškailo pulled a cot next to his for Benca and helped him sit down. When Boškailo held a cigarette between Benca's crusty lips he seemed grateful. Benca had never been a smoker, but he started smoking in Čapljina.

Early one morning the guards announced there would be a trial. A makeshift tribunal was set up in an adjoining room. The Croats wanted to make an enemy out of Boškailo. They wanted to proclaim him a leading Bosniak organizer so they could have an explanation for the Croats who kept asking, "What happened to the doctor?"

The door opened and a judge walked in wearing long black robes. Boškailo was startled to see his friend Gordana, a beautiful, soft-spoken woman with long, straight hair whose family had moved from Belgrade, the capital of Serbia, to Čapljina. If there was one person he thought his family could turn to in a crisis, it was Gordana.

He was dumbfounded that she would agree to play judge in this kangaroo court. At first he could not speak. Then he began to shout, "After all this I will find you, Gordana, and you will be ashamed of what you've done."

Gordana looked startled and then ran out of the room crying. He might have felt sorry for her, but he was not in a position to feel sorry for anyone. Nothing could make him believe Gordana had not had a choice. What was the worst that could have happened if she had refused to be a judge? She would have lost her job. She would have found another one after the war.

Sometimes the only thing he could think about was the betrayal. They had been so close, the Bosniak and Croatian people. They shared clothes, food, coffee, beds. They visited one another's homes daily. There was a tradition in Bosnia. When two Bosnians had coffee in their homes, they left a third cup upside down in case somebody else came.

Today no one in Bosnia leaves a third cup.

Just two prisoners kept up their ritual of praying five times a day. They would spread their clothes like a prayer mat, turn toward Mecca, and fall to their knees, invoking the name of Allah while the others sat and watched.

They had not always been religious men, these two. They had discovered the prayers late in life and had embraced Islam with a convert's fervor.

The other men asked them not to pray so openly, saying they risked upsetting the guards and putting all their lives in danger. But the two men were determined to show their righteousness whatever the cost.

During Ramadan all the men took a risk when they started to fast without discussing it first. They would save up food at lunchtime and dinner and eat it after sundown. The guards could not force them to eat during the day, and that was the beauty of the month.

If truth be told, few Bosnian Muslims were observant. Few prayed five times a day. They practiced Islam through celebration rather than daily routine, Boškailo liked to say, through enjoyment rather than fear of God.

Boškailo's generation studied philosophy in school and read all about Sufism and mysticism. When people asked Boškailo how he felt about his religion, he said, "I belong to the cosmos." He had never divided the world into believers and atheists. People had all sorts of ways of finding meaning. Some people believed in a higher justice. He believed in a higher power or organization of the world. He could not comprehend how the world was organized. But he believed in equilibrium, a balance. He believed in this strongly.

Boškailo had not prayed at home. But he found himself praying each night in the camp.

He did not think he had anything to say to God. So he said a prayer for dead people. Every day he would add more and more people. It helped him fall asleep. He prayed for people who had died during the war, and for those who had died before. His young brother who had died many years earlier in an accident. His father, who had died six months before the war. Then his grandparents, all four of them.

There was no way he would miss that prayer. At the time the only logic was that he had prayed the night before and he was still alive the next morning. He was convinced that if he did not say the prayer, he might not make it through another day.

In war, one had to be superstitious.

He did not know whether the others were becoming more or less disillusioned with religion as the days wore on. He just knew that one night when a man began chanting from the Koran, a dozen men joined in. Then two dozen. Then fifty. Soon more than one hundred men were chanting in Arabic.

And no one said a word about it later.

———

One evening, after the doors were locked, Boškailo heard people arguing outside. Two men hoisted him on their shoulders so he could open the window and see who was there. He spotted an unfamiliar woman standing outside the window. She was speaking German, and a man, a stranger, was interpreting for her. Boškailo guessed they were from the International Committee of the Red Cross.

The interpreter said they knew this was a concentration camp holding prisoners.

"There are no prisoners here," Boko replied.

Fortunately, the man looked up and saw Boškailo's face in the window. Boškailo held up a pack of cigarettes, a well-known brand: Filter 160. The number 160 was at least an inch tall.

The man thought Boškailo was requesting cigarettes, and he asked Boko if he could leave some for the prisoners.

Boškailo held up the pack and pointed to the number 160. The man looked confused, but Boškailo kept pointing to the number as if he were leading a game of charades. Finally, the man gave the Boškailo the high-five sign. He got it: there were about 160 prisoners in Čapljina.

After much prodding, Boko allowed the man into their quarters, and he handed out identification cards to each prisoner.

"Please fill in your name, date of birth, and the date you were arrested," he said.

It did not mean they would be released. It did not mean the guards would not beat them. But when the men went to sleep that night, they felt hopeful they would not be killed.

———

The following week, the guards ordered fifty men to board a bus for Gabela, a former army training camp in a town a couple of miles south of Čapljina. Boko did not want the International Committee of the Red Cross to find the prisoners it had registered or the new ones who had since arrived. So he emptied the camp and opened a new one.

As soon as the bus arrived at Gabela, he herded the men into a white stucco building that housed their new quarters: a large windowless room with scraps of carpet covering the floor. Boškailo, the dentist, and the professor staked out spots on the ground and rolled up the loose clothing they carried in plastic bags to make pillows.

They hid what little money they had left in cigarette packs and underwear. Perhaps Boko approved of their little underground economy. He had never tried to confiscate the small bills prisoners used to pay the guards to get them cigarettes, honey, powdered juice, and chamomile tea.

They were always able to get cigarettes. The most violent guards would sell them cigarettes for a little cash. The good-hearted guards slipped them cigarettes for free.

But in Gabela, Boko grew tired of seeing the smoke seeping through a small opening in the prisoners' quarters. One day he came inside with his gun.

"If you light up one more cigarette, I will shoot you," he said.

Boko closed the door behind him and no one spoke. Then one man after another lit his cigarette. Within ten minutes all fifty of them were smoking.

It was a stupid move, Boškailo thought, an incredibly stupid move. But if it happened again, they would do it again.

At night, the men took some comfort in sleeping near one another, their arms and legs touching in the cramped space. They would talk until two or three in the morning, or if they could not sleep, they would get up to smoke cigarettes laced with chamomile tea, a trick they had learned from a man who had been in prison. When they finally fell asleep, they slept in unison, seven big guys all in a row. When one man turned to the right, the rest turned to the right. When one man turned to the left, they all turned to the left. It felt safer that way.

Staying asleep was harder. Boškailo would wake up in the middle of the night to the sound of a man screaming or insomniacs smoking and talking in a corner. And he would be startled to see a man's body next to his.

———

In Gabela, he began the little rebellions that kept him sane. He refused to eat camp food. No visitors were allowed, no one brought food, and so he got thinner and thinner until his clothes hung on him. He would not let them shave him, so his long beard covered his gaunt face. Being hungry for ten or fifteen days was no big deal. Being thirsty for three or four days—he would never like to have that feeling again.

But he still had some strength. In the mornings, the guards put the prisoners on buses and dropped them off at farms where they loaded hay. One day when he was working on a farm, a group of Bosniak women in the distance called him to eat with them. He left the group and joined the women because he hoped they would get news to his family.

When the women heard the guards calling Boškailo, they got scared, and he left before he could bring them trouble.

Afterward he walked by the nearby River Krupa, and he could not resist. He took off all his clothes and jumped into the water. The guards were calling him and waving their arms. But he was not paying attention. He swam in the clear, cool water.

The guards threatened him when he got back to the bus. He would not be allowed out, they told him. He would be transferred to a stricter camp. But he was high from his little escapade, and he did not care. On the ride back to the camp, he opened the windows and sang an old Bosnian song that the Croats particularly hated, about a Bosnian girl, Mejra, who is carried on a wooden plank on which Muslim corpses are buried. A dinner awaits her in heaven with the beautiful girls, Huriyas.

> Water ran
> From hill to hill
> Carried Mejra on *tabut*
> Come on, Mejra
> Come and dine with us
> Dine and don't wait for me
> Awaiting me
> Is a finished dinner
> In Heaven among *huriyas*
> Give saalam
> To my dear old mother
> Tell her to pray five times a day
> Tell her to fast
> The month of Ramadan
> Give *Kurban* in Mejra's name.

He sang his song again and again until he was too tired to sing.

CHAPTER 6

Beyond Our God

From bad to bad from mad to mad
Beyond our thoughts beyond our god
—Mak Dizdar

Boko followed the men like a tick that was becoming ever more bloated.

"Big Doctor," Boko would say to Boškailo in a loud voice. "Come here.

"You are a friend of the Bosnian president," he would claim, though Boškailo had never met the man. And Boko would accuse him of being a leader in the anti-Croatian movement who needed to be stopped.

In the first camp the men had not thought much about Boko. He was a fat man approaching fifty with no life outside the camp. The prisoners were his only source of companionship. They would make fun of him, but they would be nice to him so he would let them sleep with the door open or bring them a few cigarettes. He was almost apologetic about having to keep them in line.

The transformation took a few months. It was probably one of those things that happened to guards in all concentration camps. Initially they were not sure how far they could go. Then they got more and more power, and they were not able to manage that power. Boko became a man without feeling.

One afternoon he ordered some of the prisoners to go outside and lie on the hundred-degree asphalt for several hours. Men came in with second- and third-degree burns, covered in dirt.

Another morning he ordered Boškailo to stand near a wall in the barracks, seven or eight yards from him. While Boškailo was frozen in position, Boko pointed his gun at him and shot. As in the movies, pictures of his family flashed inside Boškailo's head until he realized that Boko had missed, and the bullet had passed between his legs.

"I missed you today. I'll try again tomorrow. I'll be here at seven."

That night Boškailo's friends told him Boko probably would not come back, but Boškailo sat up all night.

At 7 a.m. Boko opened the door and stood at the entrance with his gun.

"Big Doctor, stand up." Boškailo stood up in the middle of a sea of prisoners sitting on the floor. Why should he die this way, he asked himself. He did not want to be shot to death in Gabela by a waiter.

"I should shoot you because you organized the Bosnians," Boko said, as if Boškailo had been a major military leader.

Then Boko took a step backward and smiled. "But I don't feel like killing you today. I'll come back tomorrow."

But Boko took out his rage on a younger man, the dentist's first cousin, a handsome twenty-two-year-old who towered over Boškailo. The young man was hoping to escape, but the prisoners had agreed among themselves that they would not try to leave because the Croats would retaliate against their families.

Boškailo wished to God the young man had fled.

One day the dentist's cousin came back from a work assignment with a piece of bread under his cap. Boko came in and searched several prisoners he suspected of hoarding food. He found the cousin's bread and ordered him to go to the military post nearby. There Boko shot the young man and watched him as he bled to death.

Boškailo remembers best one particular guard from Gabela. While Boko was fat and slovenly, this guard was slim and good-looking, a movie version of a military man. One afternoon he and Boškailo were making small talk when the guard suddenly became serious. He told him that soon all Bosnians would be sent to Zenica, a smoggy industrial city in the center of the country.

"Why Zenica?" Boškailo asked.

This area was going to be "ethnically cleansed" of Bosnians, the guard said. Boškailo could not tell if the man was pleased by the news or just resigned.

When Boškailo returned to the barracks and told his friends, several said they did not believe him. Some of them refused to talk to him, convinced he was trying to start trouble. But that was the moment, Boškailo saw, when the prisoners came out of their trances. The war was not going to end tomorrow. And they were not going home anytime soon.

———

In late June, the guards shoved thirteen prisoners from Gabela into a truck and took them twenty miles away to the Heliodrome, just outside Mostar. The camp had once been the Yugoslav army's boarding school for pilots. Blocks of huge dormitories were surrounded by miles of trees and grass.

The commander was waiting for them at the door: a stocky man in his fifties with thick black hair and brows knitted together. Boškailo recognized him. He was not a career military man, but an accordionist who had played in the café bars.

He took away the prisoners' personal items. Still, Boškailo managed to hold on to a medical book and his toothpaste tube, which he used to hide money in by slitting the wide end open. Fortunately, the guards did not check their underwear, so no one noticed the small radio Boškailo hid in his pants.

The guards directed the dentist to the first floor. They sent Boškailo to one of three big rooms on the second. On the door, Boškailo saw, someone had scrawled graffiti: "Is someone crazy here or what?" He liked that.

Their quarters had a bathroom—that was the good news. But there was no shower, and the stench of men who had not bathed in months filled the air.

Twenty men had arrived earlier. The mayor of Mostar was there. So was Džemo, the editor in chief of a major Bosnian magazine, as well as another journalist. Boškailo was more surprised to see Vlado and Rudi, two Bosnian Croats. He had heard that they had refused to serve in the Croatian army because they did not want to fight against their friends.

The men were less afraid of the guards than of their fellow prisoners in the room next door. They were Croatian: petty thieves who had stolen from the Croatian army, as well as drug addicts and murderers. And they had a steady supply of alcohol.

The Croats would sleep all day and drink all night—then go next door, take what food and clothing they wanted, and kick whomever they felt like goading. Some of the Bosnians were too weak to resist. But Boškailo frightened even the most inebriated men when he threatened to kill them in their sleep.

He was lucky enough to get a bed, and he kept his radio in his pillow, though the guards had threatened to kill anyone with a radio. He would touch the batteries to a warm tin surface so they would heat up and recharge.

The men would pass around the radio at night. One person at a time would listen to the news with the volume so low the guards could not hear. Later, to fool the guards, they would sit on the floor and play cards, and relay the news as if talking about their dreams.

"I had a dream the Bosnian army took control of the city of . . ."

"I had a dream the Croatian army retreated."

When Goran, the journalist, told the men he had a dream the Croatian army had taken control of Mostar and everyone had been evacuated, he had a hard time convincing them it was just a dream.

During the day the guards put the prisoners to work. In the morning, they called the names of those who would be sent to the front to be used as human shields and forced labor. Mostar was a city with one street dividing the Bosniak and Croatian soldiers. The prisoners would be lined up in front of the Croatian soldiers so the Bosniaks would not shoot, and sometimes the prisoners came back to the Heliodrome prison covered in other men's blood. Boškailo was awaiting his turn when the war changed course.

On June 30, 1993, the Bosnian army took part of Mostar. The Croatian army responded with an order to force all Bosniaks living on the other side of the river to leave. They picked up Bosniaks in the streets and entered apartments by force, giving people seconds to get out. In two days, they ethnically cleansed Mostar.

Women and men were brought to the camp by the hundreds, until thousands of people were crammed into the army buildings. Through the window, Boškailo and the others could see the people standing shoulder to shoulder in the gym, a holding pen for new prisoners, and even at a distance they could recognize faces.

"Oh my God, that's my professor!"

"That's my cousin Kemal!"

What shocked Boškailo most was how few guards were watching all the prisoners. He saw one guard standing in the gym holding a megaphone and threatening hundreds of Bosniaks.

Why didn't anyone rise up, he wondered. It did not make sense, one guard terrorizing so many men and women. Why didn't someone grab his megaphone and topple him? But he knew the answer. Like him, they were afraid for their families.

The phrase "ethnic cleansing" took on new meaning. Within months, the last civilians would be kicked out of their houses, forced to leave behind pictures and treasures, and sent to foreign countries with whatever reminders of home they could fit into plastic bags.

———

At night the prisoners sang sevdah. If the guy next to Boškailo knew a sevdah he did not know, he would teach Boškailo. Then Boškailo would teach the man one he knew. They sang for hours.

> Mother was waking up Sejdefa
> Wake up, my daughter Sejdefa.
> Sun has long risen
> Morning has long dawned.
> You think, mother
> That I am sleeping.
> I am young, parting with my soul.
> Call for me, mother
> A doctor,
> And my first love.

Oh how we looked at each other
On a boat in the sea,
The illness could be cured.

During these times, Boškailo thought, the men did not feel pain when they heard the cries of men being tortured. A person must be peaceful when singing sevdah.

The guards took away their freedom, their families, their books, Boškailo thought, but they could not take away their sevdah. They could keep them standing naked for hours and force them to defecate in front of each other. But the guards could not touch their thoughts.

Every day Boškailo looked forward to the quiet moments before he went to sleep at night. That was when he would think of his family.

His wife had always been there because she was his wife. In the camp, he realized how much she meant to him.

"I could not imagine myself coming home. I could not see myself standing in my house. But I would picture myself with Aiša, Timur, and Mak in an idyllic place somewhere far away by the water. I would lie there and think about how we were going to be together again. Sometimes I had to force myself to stay awake just so I could have a few more moments with Aiša. This dream of mine kept me sane; it kept me happy. It was an illusion, but it was mine."

————

There were many ways to kill yourself in a camp. You could provoke a guard so he shot you. You could inflict physical harm on your own body.

When Boškailo noticed a sudden change in a man in his early forties who had already lost his son and brother in the war, he started watching him more closely. First, the man stopped sleeping. Next, he stopped talking.

Then Boškailo saw the scars. The man was waking up each morning with bite marks on his arms. He was trying to bite himself to death at night.

That's when Boškailo started talking to men in trouble when everyone else was asleep. Two other doctors in the room worked during the day tending to wounds of the body. Boškailo was not a psychiatrist yet, but he worked late at night tending to wounds of the psyche.

He did not know how to make sense of the war, let alone begin to talk about healing in a dark army barracks. He could not explain why people they had considered their friends had turned on them. He could not make promises like, You will see your wife soon.

He did not want to offer pat answers to this man about faith. But he knew the man came from a fairly religious family, so he told him it was God's business when it was his time to die. And that he had a duty to God, his family members, and his fellow prisoners to survive.

"We need you in the group," Boškailo told him. "We have to stick together."

It was little to offer, but the man stopped the biting when he started talking. And when he woke in the mornings he seemed a little more at peace.

"Did God ever intervene?" Boškailo asked when we spoke. "I do not know, but there were some things I could not explain. Why, for example, when we were in crowded cells and had to eat near the can we defecated in and never washed our hands, did no one get sick? 'Doctor, explain it to me,' people would ask. I could not explain.

"But why would God keep a few of us healthy and fail to intervene on behalf of the tens of thousands of Bosnians who were killed? I do not have an answer. I do not even try to find an answer to that question.

"Some people would say, 'There must be a reason for this.' That always enraged me. How could they even say it? Did anyone really believe we were being punished for not being good Muslims? Or that the Holocaust happened because Jews were not good Jews?

"It is not okay to say that thousands or millions of people were put to death for a reason. You either have to be crazy to say that, or you have never seen a good man die young."

———

Jusuf "Juka" Prazina was the soldier Boškailo feared most. He had been a Bosniak warlord in his twenties and was lauded as a hero throughout the country when he defended Sarajevo against the Serbs. Then he became involved in organized crime, heading a racketeering ring, and was wanted by the government. So he jumped ship and joined the Croatian army.

He arrived at the Heliodrome in late June 1993. He looked like Charles Bronson, only with more wrinkles, Boškailo thought, and he walked with a limp. Beside him walked a big German shepherd. Juka was unarmed, but a large gun was strapped to the dog's back.

Boškailo heard from another guard that Juka was asking for him to come into the hallway. Boškailo was scared, but you did not say no to Charles Bronson.

As Boškailo walked into the hallway, Juka threw a carton of cigarettes on the floor near him. It was his way of giving a gift.

"Good," Juka said. "I need a good doctor. I'll come by at 6 a.m. Be ready."

That night, Goran told Boškailo he had to escape after Juka's appointment. Boškailo said he would follow Juka, and when he was not looking run away.

Juka did not appear in the morning, which meant that he must have been caught in the middle of a battle. Boškailo was safe for another day, and he was struck again by the randomness of it all. Any illusion he had ever had about being in control of the smallest things was gone. The only thing he could control was his own actions, and he was determined not to become like the guards he despised.

His respite was short-lived. At 8 a.m. a guard called him and several other prisoners and told them to leave the building. The prisoners were boarded on several buses and told to keep their heads down.

Boškailo's driver drove for at least three hours, Boškailo figured, and he had no idea where they were going.

"We're headed for Šurmanci," a prisoner in back whispered.

Šurmanci, Boškailo thought. His grandparents had refused to talk about Šurmanci. Not until high school did he learn of the natural pits just outside Šurmanci, across the river from Počitelj. During World War II, the Croatian Ustasha brought hundreds of Serbian women and children from the village Prebilovci to the largest pit, Golubinka, and threw them inside. Some were killed during the fall. Others suffocated later under the bodies. Witnesses still recall the children's screams. And Serbian nationalists continually point to Šurmanci as a reason to fight.

Šurmanci was only a few minutes away from the camp. Perhaps the driver had been going in circles to confuse them.

"We are above Šurmanci on the hill," whispered a prisoner who had risked a glance out the window.

The bus stopped suddenly.

"Get out," a guard shouted, and the men disembarked slowly. For twenty minutes they stood in silence, looking at the ground and imagining falling into the abyss.

Then two of the guards started arguing, about what the prisoners could not tell.

"Get back on the bus," one of them shouted.

"You're out of luck. You're headed for Dretelj."

CHAPTER 7
This Corner of Grief

We have crept into this corner of grief,
turning the water wheel into a flow of tears.
　　　—Rumi

They survived the hell—
who held each other's hands
man beside man
　　　　—Ilija Ladin, Bosnian poet (1929–)

Dretelj was a former Yugoslav army barracks with aluminum hangars and five brick buildings in a suburb of Čapljina. Several months earlier, Croats had held Serbs here. Now it was the Bosnians' turn.

Boškailo smelled the burning paper first as he entered the receiving station. Then he saw the huge pile of ID cards burning in a vat.

Hivzo said they were stealing their identities, but Boškailo did not care much about documents. The clean-shaven, short-haired men in the pictures did not look much like them anyway. Now their unwashed hair was down to their shoulders; their beards were long and straggly. The guards could cut their hair and shave them. But those who entered Dretelj would never be the same.

Once again, the guards strip-searched them and tried to confiscate everything. This time the guards took nitroglycerin from a man who had had a heart attack. He died four days later.

Boškailo wanted to hold on to one thing he had never hidden from the guards: his book on internal medicine. It was of no danger to anyone. He had carried it with him from camp to camp in the hope that one day he would be a doctor again.

He was thrilled when he recognized a guard walking toward

him. He had been Boškailo's patient three years earlier, when he was in his late twenties. He could not have children, and he did not have much money. But Boškailo was able to get him to see one of the best fertility doctors in Europe.

"Hi, Doctor. How is everything?"

"If I need something, may I call you?" Boškailo said in a low voice. "Can you help me contact my wife and kids?"

The guard told him to keep quiet and grabbed his book from his arms. He took away the only thing that connected Boškailo to the outside world.

Some prisoners managed to hold on to their valuables, like wedding rings and watches, which, in a pinch, they could sell to the guards for twenty German marks (the equivalent of twenty dollars), the cost of a carton of cigarettes. One man held a $100 bill folded into tiny pieces in his hand. The guards turned him around five times during the search, but they did not find his money.

The guards brought the men to the aluminum hangar. It was late June and more than ninety degrees outside, so inside it was sweltering. Boškailo saw about one hundred men in various stages of undress. As he drew closer he saw they were putting on heavy Serbian uniforms. In the height of the afternoon heat, the guards were making them wear surplus enemy garb to humiliate them.

"Doctor," he heard a man call out. He knew many of the men from the front line. But he did not talk to anyone until he had staked out a place in a corner of the bare concrete. Then it was his spot. Nobody could take it.

The professor sat down beside him. Goran, the journalist, came next. That night they slept on the concrete without a blanket in the blistering heat. Some people had brought in grass to sleep on, but when the grass rotted, it stank. Added to the smell of unwashed bodies, it was nearly unbearable.

In the beginning, they were allowed to go outside the hangar. But they did not have a bathroom. The guards put the men next to each other in a line and told them to urinate in the canal.

They were the lucky ones. Their hangar was a hotel compared

to the special cell where people were taken to be interrogated. Prisoners were forced to stand or lie down in knee-deep water and endure beatings several times a day. Sometimes the guards beat the prisoners to death with baseball bats. Boškailo could barely recognize a cousin when he returned from solitary with gashes on his face and body.

The guards fed Boškailo's group twice a day, then once a day. One man after another had to use the same plate, whether he had tuberculosis or some other infectious disease. A man had ten seconds to eat a dollop of rice or potato in very hot water and a small piece of bread. If he did not keep his head down, the guards would kick him in the back with their boots.

The guards seemed to like meal time and sleep time best for torture. All day, prisoners looked forward to eating and sleeping. The guards tried to steal their simplest pleasures.

Sometimes the guards tormented a prisoner just for their amusement. One prisoner, Ramiz, was an openly gay singer known for his beautiful, high-pitched voice. Many people considered him one of the best sevdah singers in the region. He rarely sang in the camp, and the other prisoners were too polite to ask. But occasionally he sang softly to himself, and the others strained to listen.

Early one morning a guard asked the skinny singer to come outside.

"Sit," the guard ordered, pointing to a large rock. The singer sat. Then the guard lifted his gun and pointed it at the singer's head. "Sing," he said. The singer looked up, confused. "Sing."

He began singing softly a well-known sevdah about his beloved Bosnia, a song sure to incur the wrath of the guards.

> My Bosnia, beautiful country
> You are full of nice girls and boys
> And nice rivers and mountains.

"Louder," the guard said.
He sang louder.

The prisoners gathered by the door of the hanger, horrified that the singer was being humiliated, and yet so moved by his song that some men began to cry.

Soon the guard was joined by other guards who began firing their guns in the air, as if to applaud. When a bullet hit the singer's arm, the guard ordered him to ignore the blood dripping into the ground.

"Keep singing."

> My Bosnia, beautiful country
> You are full of nice girls and boys.

The singer survived, thanks to another prisoner who removed the bullet, but a shy performer became more withdrawn. And he stopped singing, even to himself.

Occasionally the toughest guards took a moment to reflect on what might await them after the war. Some acknowledged the possibility of life after Dretelj, of a time when they might not be wearing a uniform that gave them license to kill on a whim.

"You know, Doc," one guard said to Boškailo. "After all this is over, you will be free, and I'll be on the run in Argentina."

———

A famous prisoner in Dretelj was known as Bunda, or Big Bear. He was a burly man with blond hair and blue eyes who for fifteen years had been a patient at the largest psychiatric hospital in Sarajevo. Then the war started and the hospital could not feed its patients, so they just released them. Or they escaped. Boškailo could tell Bunda was schizophrenic, obviously hallucinating. He was always talking about voices.

He was a prisoner just like the others. But the guards realized he was crazy and therefore malleable. They would tell him to go and kick somebody, and he would. They did not give him medicine, and they fed him extra food and steroids to bulk him up. They made him do hundreds of push-ups a day to get his reward of more food. Soon he looked like a professional bodybuilder, while the rest of the men were shrinking. Boškailo had already lost one hundred pounds, and what few clothes he had were now huge.

In the afternoons Bunda would come into their hangar. He never wore a shirt, so they could see his muscles. And he wore sneakers, while the other prisoners had no shoes.

He would stand at the entrance while about five hundred men sat on the floor. They were so weak they could not stand. During the day it was 110 degrees, and their sweat was like running water on cement.

One afternoon Bunda called Boškailo.

"Doctor, it's your day. I want some money."

"I'm not giving you money, Bunda," Boškailo said. He was about thirty yards from the entrance, and when Bunda began walking toward him everyone was scared.

Two young guys stood up and told Bunda he had better not touch the doctor. Then five more men stood up. Then everybody stood up so there were five hundred people between Boškailo and Bunda.

Then Bunda left.

That night it was all they could talk about. They had beaten back Bunda.

But if Bunda had been frightened, he had not been tamed. One afternoon the men heard loud screams from outside the hangar. They saw that Bunda was fighting with a group of prisoners. He was punching them with his bare fists and kicking them when they were on the ground. A guard handed him a baseball bat, and he flung it madly until he had bashed in the heads of several of his Bosniak brothers. Four people were killed, including Omer, Boškailo's classmate from high school, and Emir, the son of a hairdresser.

When Boškailo heard later that Bunda had been found hanging in a cell in Gabela, he did not much care whether he had killed himself or someone else had done the job.

Emotional blunting, the psychiatrists call it: when people who experience trauma cease to feel happiness or sadness in order to defend themselves against the horror.

"But I never blamed Bunda," Boškailo told me. "As a physician

I always saw him as mentally ill. He was like an animal that did push-ups for food. The Croats created him."

———

A few days after Boškailo arrived at Dretelj, a guard came to tell him another prisoner had had a heart attack. The guard ordered Boškailo to go with him and the prisoner to the emergency room at the Čapljina hospital, where Boškailo had worked for years.

He was not used to being outside a camp, let alone in his emergency room, a large space divided into two areas—one for examination and one for surgery. The guard escorted the patient to the examination area and placed him on the table.

Boškailo recognized the doctor in the surgical area, Jagoda, a friend with dark hair worn short, unusual for a Bosnian woman. She was leaning over a patient on a gurney, and Boškailo noticed that the patient was badly beaten up and had a gash under his left eye. He was shaking.

"Don't go there," a policeman told Boškailo.

"I need his help," Jagoda said to the policeman.

Boškailo walked over to the bleeding man and gasped. It was his old friend Kapa. He could not believe it. He had not seen him in three months, but not a day went by that he did not miss him.

"Kapa, what did they do to you?" Boškailo whispered.

Boškailo asked a doctor if he could stitch Kapa's wound, if only to have a few moments with his childhood friend.

Kapa was disoriented but awake.

"I'm done," Kapa told him. "I'm done. They're going to kill me."

"He needs another doctor," Boškailo shouted, but the guards were already grabbing his arms to push him out of the room. He kept his eyes on Kapa until the last moment.

"I'm done," Kapa said. "Take care of yourself."

That evening when the guard brought Boškailo back to the camp, Boškailo begged him to find some news about Kapa. It turned out that when the Croatian army surrounded Počitelj, Kapa had only fifty soldiers. The Croats had rounded up the women and children and put guns and knives to their heads. If

Kapa had resisted, the soldiers would have killed the civilians, so Kapa surrendered and they took him to the police station.

The next morning, Boškailo learned that Kapa had survived the beating and had been taken back to the Čapljina station. But in the middle of the night a guard came into the building and shot him. After putting forty bullets in his body, the guard threw him in the river.

"I kept going because I always kept going," Boškailo said to me. "But I no longer placed much stock in predictions about when the war would end and who would come out alive. And late at night I stopped imagining a more peaceful time when I would sit in a café bar drinking coffee with my friend."

———

It was only natural in such a state that Boškailo should turn his thoughts to his uncle. He liked to tell the others about Bećir, if only so they would know he was family. Boškailo enjoyed one story in particular. During the war against the Serbs, his uncle was so famous for his generosity that a leading Croatian Catholic priest had asked Bećir if he could kiss his feet. Bećir said he did not deserve it. But the priest was not deterred. He grabbed Bećir's legs and kissed his feet.

One morning, a guard told Boškailo he had news of Bećir, and Boškailo's chest tightened when he detected sympathy in the guard's voice.

A group of armed Croatian soldiers, the guard told him, had gone from house to house in Počitelj rounding up Bosniaks. When Bećir went up to the soldiers to question them about their mission, a man from behind put a gun to his back.

There was no talk, no negotiation. The men Boškailo had once called friends killed the man he called his father.

His friends tried to comfort him, but what was there to say?

In his early thirties, he had already lost his father, his best friend, his uncle, and his young brother. During his evening prayers he added more names to his list.

———

He could not forgive even the kindest guards. They could have chosen not to serve as guards, not to torture people, not to shoot them. Still, he needed them to be his eyes and ears, and it was a guard who brought news of Aiša.

His wife, mother, and children had been arrested at their home in Počitelj, the guard told him, where they had been living since the Bosniaks took back the town in June.

They were taken, along with a dozen women and children, including the wife of a Bosnian commander, to a house that had been converted into a camp. They were not permitted to leave the house, but they had food and they could bathe.

"I am watching them," the guard said. "I will do everything I can to keep you informed."

Boškailo did not know what to think about the news. He was elated to know the whereabouts of his family, but horrified that they were living in a camp. Weeks went by with little information. The guard reported intermittently, but he did not know much, just that Boškailo's family was getting by and they still had enough food.

Then one day the guard told him that another guard had come to the house and told Aiša, his mother, and the children to pack up their things and get into his car. They were going to a camp in Silos.

As the guard was driving, Boškailo's mother asked him whether he knew her son, Esad, the doctor. The guard looked stunned. He stopped the car as if to rethink his strategy.

Did they have passports, he asked. Yes, they had Bosnian passports and visas to go to either Spain or Italy.

They would not be going to Silos after all. The guard said he would take them to a bus station in Čapljina in time to catch a bus to Split, Croatia. They could get from there to Italy, but there would be checkpoints everywhere. Aiša said they were willing to risk it.

They caught the bus, spent the night in Split, and took the ferry to Italy. By the time Boškailo heard the news, they were living with his sister in Pescara.

———

He tried to think of his family but could not. A symptom of post-traumatic stress disorder, he would later learn, is a sense of a foreshortened future. You cannot see your future. The idea of freedom is so overwhelming for your brain, you cannot think clearly.

By the end of July, thousands of men were locked in hangars throughout Dretelj. Boškailo spent his days sitting in a corner. He was too tired to walk. The men were so filthy that little insects were crawling on their skin and eating their flesh. They had nothing to do but wait.

Kapa was gone. Boškailo had to have someone to rely on, and it was Hivzo, the chemistry professor. Hivzo liked to tell jokes. He liked to play cards. He made them out of paper. Boškailo had never been big for card games, but he played cards all day for cigarettes. One game would last half an hour.

Boškailo was sitting outside on one of the better days when a Croatian guard in his fifties approached him. He had been one of his patients and had been working in the gas station in his town. They had always talked a little back then. They had visited one another's houses. In the camp, the guard did not say much to Boškailo, but on this day he handed him a package of figs and grapes, delicacies in Bosnia, foods you would give to a good friend. Other than that, the guard never made contact. If Boškailo called his name, he would look away. But one time Boškailo called the guard's name and he started to cry. A guard in a concentration camp was crying because of him. Boškailo would have cried with him, but he could not cry.

––––––

Then came July 13, 1993, and everything changed for the worse. The Croatian Defense Council suffered enormous losses against the Bosnian army on the battlefield. The next morning the prisoners asked the guards to let them out of the hangars so they could urinate in the canals. But the guards would not open the doors, so they had to relieve themselves in the hangar. Some men got so thirsty they drank their own urine.

For three days after the Croatian army's losses, the guards would not let the prisoners leave the hangar. They had no water or food, and the temperature was rising.

Finally, several of them banged on the hangar walls. That was when the shooting came, as if out of nowhere. Guards on the outside began shooting with machine guns into the hangar.

The men got down on their stomachs and covered their heads with plastic bags filled with underwear and T-shirts, as if they could stop bullets.

Hamo, who was on the left of Boškailo, was hit in the back of the head with two bullets. Sejo, lying on his other side, was struck in the shoulder.

The men were bleeding and screaming in pain when suddenly the shooting stopped. A couple of people brought blankets to hide the wounded from the guards. Some of the prisoners had been taken to the camp straight from army units, so they still had their first-aid kits with dressings. Boškailo had a nail clipper. Somebody brought a cigarette lighter so he could sterilize it. One by one the wounded crawled over to him or the men would carry them, and he picked fragments out of arms and hands with his fingers, which was not difficult given that the men were emaciated: all skin and a little muscle.

For deeper wounds he would operate at night while a man held a blanket over him and another held a cigarette lighter. He would cut open the skin with a razor blade and take the fragments out with a needle and the nail clipper.

Remarkably, given the shape they were in, Hamo and Sejo survived.

By day Boškailo no longer had the strength to move in the heat. He was lying down, urinating and defecating in place. In the beginning they all relieved themselves in one corner, but later they could no longer get there. Nobody was able to move.

On Day Four, the guards brought in sixty liters of water for six hundred people. Boškailo urged the men to drink their small portion slowly to avoid getting sick. One man gulped his and collapsed instantly. Then the shooting began again.

Boškailo continued to take out the fragments in a trancelike state.

"You know how many were killed in Dretelj? I cannot tell you how many. They broke thousands of bones, destroyed thousands of kidneys. And nobody came out normal."

"I know it was not Auschwitz. But who said that Auschwitz is the benchmark for terror? Do we need another Auschwitz for the world to intervene?

"Why didn't the United States and the international community help us earlier? Where was the United Nations when news reporters were broadcasting stories of atrocities occurring throughout the country, when emaciated men and women were wasting away in camps?

"Wasn't it bad enough in Bosnia to deserve a more significant UN presence? Did we need another Auschwitz before the United Nations would send peacekeepers who had the means to keep the peace?

"A couple of years after getting out of the concentration camps, I met a man and wife who had survived Auschwitz, and there was an immediate and unspoken recognition. When we sat down to talk it was as if we were the only ones in the room. They wanted to know everything about camp life. Did we have bathrooms in the barracks? How many minutes were we given to eat scalding soup? Did we get wounds in our mouths? Did the guards come in at night and hit people? When a guard came into the barracks and pointed out a man, did we know he would be taken out and shot?

"Never did they ask, Was it bad enough?"

––––––––––

There were witnesses to the suffering.

According to a report by the UN High Commissioner for Refugees, Croat forces held approximately fifteen thousand Bosnian Muslims in camps and prisons in Grbavica, Dretelj, Stolac, Ljubuški, Rodoč, and a number of other places. The majority were civilians expelled from their homes.

The International Committee of the Red Cross also reported in 1993 that 650 Serbs and 579 Croats were being held by Bosnian government forces in twenty-four detention centers in the region.

Amnesty International and other human-rights groups expressed concern about Muslim civilians "and the ill-treatment and inhuman conditions to which they, together with captured

combatants, may have been exposed" while in detention camps
in Bosnia.

On Monday, September 6, 1993, delegates of the International
Committee of the Red Cross were for the first time allowed access
to Dretelj, where they found 1,428 prisoners. A British journalist
reported that 125 inmates had been sent to an undisclosed loca-
tion before the visit. Boškailo had been among four men taken to
an underground silo near Čapljina.

Representatives of the UN High Commissioner for Refugees
saw about one hundred men after they were released from Dretelj.
"Those released complained that especially during June and July
their treatment had been inhuman. They had been given hardly
any water or food, were subjected to regular and arbitrary beatings—five were reportedly killed—and there was no sanitation."

When the reporter Ed Vulliamy saw Dretelj in 1993 he described prisoners "locked away in the dank darkness of two underground hangers, facing the hillsides."

He continued: "The metal doors had been slid open for our
visit, but many men preferred to stay inside, staring as though
blind into the ether. 'We're really not allowed out,' said one. These
men had been locked in here for up to seventy-two hours at a time,
without food or water, drinking their own urine to survive.

"They all remembered the night in July 1993 when the Croat
guards got drunk and began firing through the doors—between
ten and twelve men died that night; the back wall of the hanger
was pockmarked with bullets."

CHAPTER 8

Before the Bone Cracks

Hurry, before the bone cracks, and dawn comes
Bursting our ear-drums with the screams from the street
And we suck in air mixed with hot shrapnel.
　　—Abdulah Sidran

For thirty days in the fall of 1993, Boškailo and forty-eight other men were locked in an underground silo. They sat back to back on the bare concrete floor, holding their legs against their chests, as if waiting for something to break the monotony.

Once again, the guards passed out filthy Chetnik uniforms. During the day when temperatures inside reached 120 degrees, the men would sweat in their heavy wool coats. But at night when the temperatures dropped, Boškailo was grateful that the enemy garb kept them from freezing.

In the morning, the guards threw cans of food through an opening in the roof. Sometimes the cans landed on a man's head, but at least the group had something to eat. The guards gave them a little water for drinking, and an old bucket to use as a toilet.

If the guards remained human, the prisoners had a good day. If the guards provided enough water to drink, or opened the door to the scorching cell, or took out the bucket the men defecated in, Boškailo declared it a holiday.

What did they do all day? Some men played cards. Others joined Boškailo in forming a group to recite poetry.

"Poetry group, come here!" he would shout.

And the men would trade places so the poetry group could crouch together in a circle.

Boškailo knew some poems about women and wine by the

Persian poet Omar Khayam and some about love and injustice by the Bosnian writer Aleksa Šantić. Benca, the literature professor, knew all of Šantić's poems, along with Goethe's and Baudelaire's. So they taught each other poems line by line, and the hours passed.

Benca called the group their escape from reality, and he loved the idea that uneducated men were memorizing Goethe.

The professor's uncle was the most famous poet in Bosnia, Mak Dizdar. Boškailo had named his son after Mak.

Mak had written a poem called "Blue River":

> That's where the dark river flows
> a river that is wide and deep
> it is a hundred winters wide
> it is a thousand summers deep
> its doom and gloom will never heal
> that's where the dark blue river flows
> that's where the dark blue river flows
> the river that we have to cross

The traditional interpretation was that if you had sinned in life you could not cross the bridge and would fall into the river. If you crossed the bridge you would find yourself in heaven. Boškailo said that the camp was the Blue River and they had to cross it.

The group would say over and over again: "The blue river is in front of us, and we're going to cross it. Our destiny is to cross it. No one can stop us." And soon other men, young and old, would join in.

While some prisoners were in their twenties, others were well into their seventies and eighties. The man who sat next to Boškailo was eighty-two and delirious. He always talked about World War II. He thought he was still in the war. Another prisoner, also a doctor, was taking care of him, washing him with what little water there was. The old man would not defecate in the can, but always in his pants.

Boškailo doubted he could have shown the same devotion. And when the old man died, Boškailo admitted his happiness only to himself. He no longer had to live with the stench, and after the guards removed the body he could stretch his legs for the first time in weeks.

If he had thought about it, Boškailo might have wondered what had become of his humanity. But an underground silo was no place for thinking.

One day a guard came into the cell and ordered the men to put their hands behind their heads and stand in one corner. He had come to order one of the men to empty the bucket of excrement. Boškailo recognized the guard as one of his patients and called him by name.

"Who are you?" the guard asked.

"Esad, the doctor."

"You are not Esad," the guard said. Then he ordered Boškailo to come outside so he could see him in the light. The guard saw a skeleton with long hair and a long beard, wearing a heavy Chetnik uniform on one of the hottest days of the year. Underneath it all he recognized his doctor.

"Do you need food?" he asked Boškailo.

Boškailo said that he no longer felt hunger. But when he spotted a tap in front of the silo, he asked the guard if he could wash himself. For five weeks he had been urinating and defecating without an opportunity to wash his hands. So he went to the tap and washed his hands and face in the cool running water. And when he saw his reflection in the spigot he felt sick.

He took off his clothes and washed his body. That was when a group of six Croatian women working at the nearby Lasta waffle bakery recognized him and called him by name. Soon he was rushing to put on his clothes while the women ran toward him carrying boxes of cookies.

"Doctor, is that you?" asked a woman who had been his patient. As she handed him packages over the fence she began to cry and two others followed, stunned that men were being held just yards from their bakery.

It was painful for him to have a group of women looking at his protruding ribs, but this was a fortunate moment. These women would undoubtedly tell neighbors and friends that doctors, lawyers, and professors were being tortured nearby.

Boškailo went inside and gave the cookies to men who dreamed at night of sweets.

—————

But there was always a price to pay for these moments of joy. Guards feared that the news of the prisoners would spread quickly, so they decided to move them again.

The next morning at four o'clock the men heard knocking on the door.

"You have ten seconds to get ready," a guard shouted.

Several guards pushed open the door and rounded up the men. The guards herded them like cattle outside the silo and into the back of a small truck where they stood shoulder to shoulder. Boškailo had no idea where they were going, and he was too overwhelmed to consider the possibilities.

The driver drove fast and swerved on purpose so that the men banged into one another as they tried to make out familiar landmarks. A tree. A building. A road.

They pulled into a police compound surrounded by a fifteen-foot-high cement wall in downtown Ljubuški, five miles from Čapljina. Inside the wall sat a two-story prison next to a former police station. Boškailo scoped out the scene and was relieved to see an outside faucet.

There was little else to celebrate.

Boškailo and the professor, along with eight other men, were sent to one of seven ten-by-six-foot cells with a hole the size of an eye in the door. They quickly realized they would have to lie on their sides, feet to head, on the dirty wood floor.

People made jokes: "Your feet are smellier than mine." They had to joke. Most of them had not had a shower in eight months.

At night half the group would sleep while the others stayed awake, leaning their backs against the wall.

The guards did not give the prisoners a place to urinate. Men could go without bowel movements because of the lack of food, but they had to urinate no matter how little water they drank. Somebody had an idea to urinate in a plastic soda bottle he found on the floor. The men passed the bottle around. The strongest of them, those who had any strength left, would hoist a person to a small window to pour the bottle of urine outside when the guards were not looking.

When guards did enter their cells, it was only to cause trouble for men who were in no condition to resist. One day a guard set his sights on Boškailo and stepped over the other men to reach him. Then, without warning, he lifted his leg and struck Boškailo in the face with his boot. When Boškailo spit two teeth into his hand, the guard smiled broadly.

The prisoners' fear intensified when they began hearing sounds coming from the next cell, where, they learned later, the guards were torturing two cousins from Mostar, hitting them with a gun on the back, stomach, and legs for hours that turned into days.

"When you expect someone to be tortured or killed, you feel the pain in your hair," Boškailo said. "Sometimes the screams were so loud we put our fingers in our ears. Were they going to kill them? Were they going to kill us?"

———

Still, the prisoners continued the little protests that kept them going. One day the commander of the camp said a representative from the International Committee of the Red Cross was in his office and would deliver any messages the men wrote to their families. The commander said, "I'll give you each a piece of paper. You can write messages to anyone you want." But he said he would read every single note, and if he did not like what he saw he would shoot the author.

They had an hour to write messages to friends and family, and most of the men knew to keep it simple with reports of good health.

The next day the camp commander came into their room and was laughing. "Who wrote this?" he asked. "This is really funny." Then he read the letter:

> Dear wife,
> I am in a concentration camp, the worst mother-
> fucking camp in the world, worse than anything the
> fucking fascists in the SS came up with.

It was Hivzo, the professor. Hivzo, the soft-spoken man who had never said a mean word about anyone. Hivzo, who doubted his best friend, the Croatian professor, could ever join the Croatian army. He had signed the letter!

The guards gave the professor a couple of pieces of blank paper and asked him to write a new letter. When Boškailo saw the professor's even more vituperative second missive, he grabbed the paper and wrote his own version:

> Dear wife,
> We're all fine. Love to you and the children.

One letter was amusing. Two could be suicidal.

Boškailo was able to send one note to his wife. It said only, "Happy Anniversary. Send me a picture."

The Croatian prisoners were allowed to have family visitors, and the wife of a Croatian prisoner who had refused to fight the Bosnians collected family photographs from Aiša and brought them to Boškailo. He put the pictures in his pocket, and anytime he doubted he was going to survive, he looked at the faces of Aiša and his two young children and saw a reason to fight anything, even bullets.

He had tried to get a guard to bring him an Italian language book so he could speak to people in Pescara, where his wife and children were staying, but he could not find one. Instead, he got his hands on an English-Bosnian dictionary with a section on grammar. He and a friend memorized as many words as they could and said them aloud to one another. They had no idea how to pronounce them. But they could spell like nobody's business.

———

Then after five months in Ljubuški everything changed in an instant. Again, politics intervened: peace negotiations between Bosnia and Croatia.

The guards opened the door and let the men use the bathrooms and wash their upper bodies. The professor was so giddy he took his soap and jumped into a nearby fountain in his underwear. It was ten degrees below zero.

From then on, the guards took the men outside to eat twice a day. Did they want coffee? No problem. To boil the water, a prisoner took two wires from a small light hanging on the ceiling and dipped them in a plastic soda bottle filled with water. If the two pieces had touched it could have killed him. Such was the risk a Bosnian takes for a coffee.

The guards even allowed a visitor, a Croatian man Boškailo did not recognize at first. The man told Boškailo that the guards had given him only a couple of minutes to see him. He had been Boškailo's patient before the war, and he brought him a huge bag of fresh bread with fruits and honey.

"Bread!" The only thing a Bosnian loves more than coffee is bread.

It was obvious to Boškailo that the man was in pain. His left arm was sagging.

"What happened?" Boškailo asked him. "I didn't think you had problems with your arm."

He said, "They wrapped my arm in wire and squeezed."

"Who did?" Boškailo asked.

"The Bosnians." He explained he had been a prisoner of war in Mostar on the Bosnian side.

"Why would you come here and give me food?"

The man looked perplexed. "Because you didn't do anything bad to me."

"Good morning, allies!" a guard shouted as he opened the door to the cell. "Get out. Relax. Smoke. Have a coffee." He brought the men cigarettes and a Croatian newspaper from January 1994.

The headline read, "Washington Peace Agreement. War between Croatia and Bosnia Is Going to Stop Immediately."

"Go out and play soccer," the guard said to a sea of uncomprehending faces.

Boškailo thought it was a joke. But it was no joke.

"We are now allies," the guard said.

Within five days the door was open all the time and cigarettes were plentiful.

Guards who had kicked them were suddenly their friends. One guard asked Boškailo to tell him honestly if he had been all that bad.

"How would I know?" Boškailo told him. "You should know what you did."

When visitors started coming, Boškailo dared hope for release. First a representative of the European Parliament arrived. Boškailo could hear the representative calling his name, and he could hear the Croatian guard replying that he was not there.

"I'm here! I'm here," Boškailo shouted.

The representative was able to make the guards open the door. He told the men that he was there to help and that in a few days they would be free.

Afterward they stayed up for several nights speculating. Was he really coming? Were they going to be released? Six days passed. Then the prisoners saw a newspaper article that said the representative had failed to get them released.

When a Swiss woman from the International Committee of the Red Cross came to visit, the men felt sure they were going to be released.

Boškailo thought he would have greeted the possibility of release with elation. Instead, he could not sleep. He wondered aloud to Benca: should he go to his family in Italy or stay home and fight?

"I thought you were a smart guy," Benca told him. "But you are really crazy. All we have left is our families. The war is over for you and me. There is no more fighting. Go home to your wife and kids."

———

A few days later, a guard knocked on the door, called Boškailo's name, and told him his days were numbered.

"We are going to shoot you. Come out. Get out."

It was his little joke.

Boškailo followed him to a cavernous room where seven or eight guards were sitting, drinking wine and whiskey and watching a Croatian musical award show on TV. His cousin, the doctor, was there, too. Just the two of them and all those guards with guns. Then a guard asked him if he wanted to make a phone call.

"The phone is out there. Call your family."

The phone was in a small office near the entrance.

"How long can I talk?"

"It's nine o'clock now. Finish before midnight."

He called and reached his family in Italy. Because he was not allowed to carry paper, he had memorized their numbers—all thirteen digits—hoping that one day he would find a phone. Aiša answered, and Boškailo told her he could hardly talk. He spoke to her, his mother, and his sister for just five minutes, betraying little emotion. That was all he could handle. Just to hear their voices, to tell them he was fine.

The impending release of the Bosniaks accounted for the sudden kindness. Soon they would be free, and the commanders and guards knew they would be called to account before some sort of international court. They knew that during World War II many Croatians and Serbs who fought on Hitler's side ended up in prison. They wanted to be remembered as the guys who gave the prisoners whiskey.

In a few days Boškailo learned there was to be a prisoner exchange in Mostar. The guards invited the men to board a truck and drove them to a real prison. From behind metal bars, the men waited for news of their fate.

Outside the building at least three hundred UN peacekeepers stood across from soldiers in the Croatian army.

Day after day Boškailo stood inside the prison, hoping that someone would shout his name. Nothing. Then one morning, the Red Cross representative called out, "Boškailo!"

He went to the door, and a Croatian guard tried to stop him

from leaving. But the representative pushed him through, and Boškailo took off running.

"Ahead of me I saw a Croatian soldier hitting a chronically mentally ill man in the face with his boot. He had been so disoriented he had not known he was in a camp. We motioned to the United Nations soldiers, who quickly intervened. It was the last torture I witnessed during the Bosniak-Croatian war."

———

For fifteen hours the men sat side by side during the ride to freedom. When their truck arrived at Gašinci, a refugee camp run by the UN High Commissioner for Refugees in northwest Croatia, they saw a virtual city of cabins and tents. Four thousand Muslims, they learned, were waiting for their travel papers to Europe or the United States.

Boškailo was free again. He could come and go as he pleased. But after the long imprisonment he had a hard time doing anything but sitting on his cot in a dark tent.

A distant relative from the nearby town of Osjek saw him interviewed on CNN upon his arrival and came to the camp to find him. Boškailo could not help but notice her startled expression. He weighed little more than a hundred pounds. And his knees were so swollen he could not walk more than a few feet. Her boyfriend helped him to the car and drove them back to her apartment house, then carried Boškailo up the stairs to her second-floor home.

He looked around at the kitchen, the dining room table, the bathroom with its modern plumbing. It was all too much, this glimpse of normal living, and he could not wait to get back to Gašinci.

Back at the camp he met briefly with a Bosniak physician to see if she could do something about his swollen knees. She was working for Doctors without Borders, which ran a small urgent-care hospital in the camp. She recommended ice and rest, as if he had not had enough rest.

A few days later, she invited him and another male doctor to go into town for pizza and beer. Boškailo told her he was sorry but he could not leave the camp.

"Are you sick?" she asked.

"I'm not well."

"Why don't you feel well?" She had seen his knees, and her question annoyed him.

"I was in concentration camps for almost a year."

"Are you going to cry your whole life because you were in a fucking concentration camp?"

So he agreed to go.

They rode in an ambulance, and he asked her why she had talked to him so harshly.

"You've got to decide to go on with your life or you'll be crying forever." She knew of what she spoke. Her parents, it turned out, had been in Sarajevo under siege without food. They had been bombed day after day.

Boškailo could have been angry, but he was not. Hearing such stories made him feel less alone.

Aiša and the children had left Italy. The UN High Commissioner for Refugees helped her and the children resettle in Chicago, where they moved in with Boškailo's cousin who had been living there since the 1950s. Boškailo wanted to go to Chicago as soon as he was healthy.

In the meantime, when he was bored in the camp he would pass by the offices of Doctors without Borders, where the Bosniak physician was working with one other doctor. Sometimes he would come in for a cup of coffee, but not to talk about the war. The doctors had told him they were fed up with war stories. Then they asked him if he would like to work as a doctor.

"You can get back to your life," they told him. And it helped him to realize he could have a life.

Boškailo began working in urgent care and was on call for fifty elderly patients in their eighties and nineties who came from a nursing home. Five days later he felt so much better physically and emotionally that he began to play basketball. When his knees acted up, women in the camp would gather ice for him and come to his cabin to help him heal.

Each day he waited for news of his future. Some days he would stand for hours in line to make a five-minute call to Aiša and the boys in Chicago. But he could hardly visualize them, let alone imagine their reunion.

Finally, Boškailo received his papers to fly to the United States. The UN High Commissioner for Refugees had arranged for him to be reunited with his family. One afternoon before he left he went to visit his cousin, a famous basketball coach, in Zagreb, Croatia. Walking down the street he ran into the guard whom he had helped get to the fertility specialist, the one who had taken his book on internal medicine. Boškailo had no idea what to do. What should he say to him?

"Everything is okay in Počitelj now," the man said. "You should come back." But how could everything be okay, Boškailo thought, when thousands of people had been ethnically cleansed?

When he arrived at his cousin's home he had a panic attack. He could not breathe; he was sweating and shaking. His cousin's mother gave him some Valium.

He returned to the refugee camps, and the night before he left for the United States, the doctors wanted him to go out for a drink to say goodbye. The next morning he would take a bus to Vienna, and from there he would fly to New York, then Chicago.

The café bar was on a main street in Zagreb lined with hundreds of outdoor cafés. There were men sitting in army uniforms, and they had guns. One was the guard from Čapljina that Boškailo had seen earlier.

He felt an electric shock through his head when the guard stood up and approached him.

"How are you, Boškailo? What's new?"

"Actually, I'm leaving for the United States," Boškailo told him. "My family is there. For a while you're not going to see me. But when I come back to my town I'll be driving a tank, and the first person I shoot will be you."

Benca went back to the army. He had never intended to return to his family, Boškailo suspected. Benca had just wanted Boškailo to know it was all right to go back to his. So in August 1994, Boškailo took the bus from Zagreb to Vienna.

The next morning, two of his friends from the war who had settled in Germany were waiting at the Vienna station to see him.

"Goodbye is one of the worst things you can say," Boškailo told me. "When you spend months together talking and drinking, and the person suddenly goes to St. Louis or Chicago, you cannot just shake hands and say, 'I'll see you later.' So I hugged my friends without saying a word.

"We had at least ten concentration camp survivors on the bus. But there was no reminiscing. Not until the flight from Austria to New York did the memories come flooding back. It was too much. Everyone was there. It was too much."

CHAPTER 9

Back Once More

I come back once more
Crushed
To the
Core
      —Mak Dizdar

His family was waiting for him: his wife, his boys, his mother, and a cousin, who had lived in Chicago since 1956.

"How can I describe the feeling? I was completely overwhelmed. I did cry, I will say that, but I did not want them to remember me crying. So I tried to talk to keep from crying more. And yet I could not talk.

"I left my son Timur when he was four and found him at five. My younger son, Mak, was three years old. Timur recognized me. Mak grabbed my hand and looked at my face as if he did not know me.

"'Are you my daddy?' he asked.

"Later when a Bosnian doctor came to visit, Mak said, 'I have two dads now.' Every young guy of a similar age he called Daddy.

"When we told him he could no longer share a bed with his mother, he said, 'You cannot sleep with my mom. I sleep with my mom, and you are not little.'

"My wife had been holding everything together for so many months. She had been fighting so hard for me and the kids. She walked instead of paying for bus fare so she could buy my older son a toy. Two weeks after I arrived, she just crashed. Suddenly she was lost. She was so weak I could not help her. She told me when she walked down the Chicago streets she felt as if there was a novel in her head and she was reliving the Croatian-Bosnian war. She had the feeling of choking. She lost a lot of weight. She could not eat. Finally a doctor prescribed medicine for posttraumatic stress disorder.

"For many months we talked about things of the moment without talking about feelings. Avoidance was the most important element of how we dealt with one another. What was important was just being together. I am still not sure Aiša has told me everything. We have certain things—secrets—to protect each other. Some stories of the camp I could never tell her. I will never tell her. Without explaining, we accepted the reality of losing our previous life completely. People ask me my birthday and I say August 8, 1994, in the Chicago O'Hare Airport."

They could never make up for the lost time. Boškailo and Aiša had lost those moments together. But they were close now, closer than before. His family had always been important to him. Now he loved them even more.

For months, it seemed, he lived in a haze. He was so traumatized that he did not know he was traumatized. He had the same nightmare every night. He was on the street surrounded by a hundred Americans who watched as he stabbed a Croatian guard. Everybody was applauding and cheering him on. He would wake up in a sweat.

What had happened to his humanity with that dream?

He knew he could not kill anybody. And yet the dream felt so good. Sometimes he thought the only reason he wanted to live was to get revenge.

What little hope Boškailo had for peace was shattered in July 1995 when Bosnian Serb forces overran Srebrenica, another UN "safe area." Despite the presence of 450 lightly armed Dutch peacekeepers, the Serbs came in and killed more than eight thousand Muslims and expelled some twenty thousand Muslim women, children, and elderly. Only then did Western allies promise decisive and substantial action. On August 30, NATO launched massive air strikes to stop the Serbs in the region.

Opponents, including the playwright Harold Pinter and the former U.S. attorney general Ramsey Clark, argued that Western countries had no right to impose their will on a sovereign nation. Proponents called it a humanitarian intervention in the face of a gross violation of human rights.

Boškailo and his friends believed that the international community had failed to protect the Bosniaks before, during, and after the war. World leaders, he thought, had dismissed the war as a religious and ethnic conflict. They refused to acknowledge the scale of human-rights violations, which would have required them to intervene under international law.

Then on November 21, 1995, the presidents of Bosnia, Croatia, and Serbia initialed the Dayton Peace Accords in Dayton, Ohio. Sarajevo remained the capital of Bosnia, but the agreement divided Bosnia into two autonomous, ethnically based areas: the Federation of Bosnia and Herzegovina, made up of Bosniaks and Croatians, and the Serbian Republic. The Federation was given 51 percent of the country. Serbs were given 49 percent.

Was this the Serbs' reward, Boškailo asked, for a war that left 200,000 dead and another 2.7 million refugees? How was a survivor supposed to heal knowing the aggressors had profited from their crimes?

Boškailo liked to say his education began in the winter of 1994–1995 when he met Mary Fabri. He was not ready for her when she came to the door of their Chicago apartment six months after he had arrived in the United States. She told him she was a psychologist with the Bosnian Refugee Mental Health Program. He guessed that she was in her early forties. She wore loose cotton clothing and her hair in a long braid like an American hippie.

Aiša had enrolled him in an English class as soon as he arrived. The instructors had no idea why he did so well on the written section of the placement test—he came in at level four of five—when he could not speak a word. Certainly the grammar book that he and his friend had studied at the Ljubuški prison had helped. Boškailo barely understood what Mary Fabri was saying to him, but Aiša translated.

She had heard about Boškailo from members of the Bosnian community, and she wanted him to go with her to a psychiatric hospital and interpret for a Bosnian young man who was mentally ill. He said absolutely not. She insisted. The man was only sixteen and had only his mother with him.

"He has no father," Aiša told him.

So Boškailo agreed to go.

Fabri gave him the outline of the story. During the war, the young man and his mother had had to walk over dead bodies to avoid being killed, and now he was having flashbacks.

In the car with Fabri, Boškailo did not have much to say. He had never liked psychologists much, never saw the need for them.

"How do you deal with your trauma?" she asked him.

"What trauma?" he asked her.

When they arrived at the hospital room where the young man and his mother were waiting, Boškailo regretted agreeing to assist an American woman he could barely understand.

Fabri asked Boškailo if he could speak directly to the young man, and he introduced himself as a doctor and offered a greeting in Bosnian. The young man's face brightened for a moment, but he held his arms tightly around his chest. After several minutes of silence, he started talking out of the blue about dead bodies, and Boškailo nodded his head. It was all he could do.

On the way home, Fabri told Boškailo she was sorry she could not help him when he was in a concentration camp, but she wanted to assist Bosnians who needed help now. Would he be her interpreter? Boškailo thought she was crazy. He knew only about a hundred words in English. But he asked her to call him the next time she was visiting this young man.

He was not sure why he kept coming back. He was not ready for this kind of work. But each time Fabri called, he came. In the beginning it was difficult for him to hear the stories. Although horror cannot be measured, the atrocities he had endured seemed like nothing compared to those suffered by Fabri's clients. In

Bosnia they say, "God forbid that we'll have worse." It can always be worse.

Inexperienced therapists might assume that people who had been traumatized in concentration camps would immediately trust a doctor who had come to help. But most prisoners from concentration camps, Boškailo knew, did not trust anybody. You lose trust after your neighbors become guards. You lose trust after your fellow inmates turn on you. You lose trust in humanity.

They saw one Bosnian patient from Omarska and Manjača, the most horrific Serb concentration camps, where thousands of Bosniaks and Croats had been tortured, raped, and murdered.

The patient had come to the Bosnian Refugee Mental Health Program in Chicago because his wife said that he was having flashbacks and nightmares. In the middle of the night, he would take her and the children and throw them against the wall. In the morning he would not know what he had done.

The man needed a CT scan of his head because of the injuries he had suffered, but he refused to go to the hospital, saying all the doctors in Chicago were Chetniks—Serbs.

Fabri and other clinicians had spent several weeks trying to figure out why he distrusted doctors in particular. Boškailo learned that he had been in a camp with a Serbian doctor who had murdered prisoners.

In traditional psychotherapy, he remembered from his medical school rounds, self-disclosure was not recommended. But this could be a way to reach the man.

"So I hear you were in a concentration camp for only eight or nine months," Boškailo said to the man in Bosnian. "That's nothing. I was in for twelve." The man was startled for a moment, but then he started asking questions about Boškailo's experience: Did they have beds in his camp? Did they have a bathroom?

Then the man began telling his own extraordinary story. Outside his camp, the Serbian guards had come after fifteen prisoners and tried to kill them with an ax. The man had suffered wounds to his left kidney area and was declared dead, but three days later when the other prisoners arrived under order to bury the bodies, he opened his eyes. A prisoner offered to pay the guards if they would let the man live. When the guards agreed, a group of prisoners traded in what money, watches, and jewelry they had managed to hide in exchange for this man's life.

Did a doctor need to have survived a concentration camp to treat this man? No, Boškailo thought, but during the first several sessions therapists had to work on gaining trust, by listening and making comments that showed they were listening. He learned this from watching Fabri.

A patient would say, "Why am I telling you this? You cannot imagine this." And Fabri would answer, "I was not there, but I'm here for you at this moment to listen to you and hear how you feel."

She would say, "You are the expert in the area of what happened to you. I'm here to learn from you."

Fabri did gain this man's trust through listening and helping his family, and slowly he began recovering. Six months later he had a job installing floor tiles and was making a lot of money. He sent at least a thousand dollars a month to friends and family in Bosnia. Two years later he took his family and went back to his country. Once Boškailo got a letter from him. He wrote that he still laughed that he had thought Boškailo was a Chetnik.

Sometimes Boškailo stumbled at his job as interpreter. A Bosnian woman told Fabri how Serbian soldiers came to her village. They attacked civilians, cut up their bodies, boiled the pieces in large pots, and forced her and other survivors to eat from the pot.

Boškailo stood up as if in a trance. "That's not true!" he declared.

Fabri did not know the details of what was being said, but she urged Boškailo to say something soothing to the woman, which he did. The woman seemed so relieved to have talked about her experience that she did not take much notice of Boškailo's reaction. Later she told them it was the first time she had told the story to anyone.

Boškailo liked to say that Mary Fabri tricked him into therapy. They had lunch together three or four times a week. She asked him to tell stories about the war, and over time he became more and more comfortable talking about trauma.

"Mary is a rare person," he told Aiša. "And I believe she was sent to me."

It was from Fabri that he learned that a strong relationship is a prerequisite for any type of therapy. Patients could sense early on through her body language that she was a deeply caring person.

She also was willing to go to a patient's home. One of their first clients, a woman from a remote village in Bosnia, invited Fabri to her apartment. So she and Boškailo went for a visit. Then they went every week because that was where the patient was most comfortable.

Soon they saved afternoons for home visits, and they got fat eating so much good pita. Fabri became addicted to coffee, which told Boškailo how well she had adapted to Bosnian culture.

Boškailo also saw changes in himself. Initially, he could not concentrate well enough to study for his medical boards, which he needed to pass to practice medicine in the United States. Through working with Fabri and her patients, he became more like his old self. He could read again. His mood was better.

Still, it would be many more months before he could tell his story in public without panicking. Early on, a psychiatrist at a local university asked him to talk to a group of medical students about his experience in the camps.

"There were thirty students, all young people. I was thinking, 'I can't do this.' I started to shake. Finally, I said, 'My name is Esad and I'm from Bosnia, and I was in six concentration camps.' But I could not go on. I was broken. I started to cry. I thought I would faint. I realized I had to leave the room. It was too dangerous to stay there.

"I went to a bathroom and washed my face. The psychiatrist came up to me and said, 'Don't worry. It's good. They should see it was real. It was a good experience.'

"I was broken in my heart, and it was good."

CHAPTER 10

The Hardest Strife

The one true war
The hardest strife
Is at your very
Core

  —Mak Dizdar

Boškailo had been living in the United States for a year when he picked up *Man's Search for Meaning,* the psychiatrist Viktor Frankl's account of his experiences in the Nazi concentration camps. Boškailo had avoided literature about the Holocaust for fear of triggering old memories. Now he wanted to be immersed in the stories of people who had put pen to paper in an effort to understand the unfathomable.

He could not help being struck by the similarity of all such camps and the modes of torture that were perfected by each subsequent generation. It was as if Frankl had been with them at Dretelj when the bullets flew and heard their anguish as they lay awake at night. It was as if he knew Boškailo's thoughts, how he had clung to his image of Aiša.

It was all there: the clothes, the rations, the "multitude of small torments" that made up everyday life in the camps.

Frankl talked about grown men huddling at night to fend off the cold.

He described how the most brutal prisoners were handpicked to be capos.

He marveled about the small miracles: how the sores and abrasions on the dirty hands of men who could not wash did not become infected.

He wrote about the edema suffered by nearly everyone in the camps: the swollen legs and skin stretched so tightly it was hard to bend one's knees.

He described the phase of apathy that allowed men like Boškailo to celebrate when an old man succumbed to death.

And it was as if Frankl knew about Kapa when he wrote that survival was a stroke of luck or a miracle, and that "the best of us did not return."

Frankl believed in the possibility of maintaining one's dignity even in the camp and of choosing one's attitude toward the suffering that few escape in this life. Boškailo had never told anyone, but he was secretly proud of the fact that he had never hit another man and had never tried to grab a guard's gun. He had never taken another man's food and had rarely raised his voice during month after month of frustration.

He hoped he had suffered bravely.

Frankl taught that it did not really matter what we expected from life, but rather what life expected from us. Men and women, he wrote, needed to stop asking about the meaning of life, and instead to start thinking of themselves as being questioned by life—daily and hourly. The answer was not in talk and meditation, but in right action and right conduct, whether in a school or a concentration camp.

It was Frankl's discussion of meaning that moved Boškailo most. The question of meaning was both philosophical and practical, and applied to survivors of all kinds of trauma, from torture to divorce. Meaning was about the big questions, the larger purpose of life and why we are here, but it also came down to the basics: Why do we get up in the morning? How do we define a successful life? What do we hope to accomplish before we die, and how do we want to be remembered?

Boškailo agreed with Frankl that meaning could be found in spite of suffering and that suffering should be avoided whenever possible, whether through political action or medical intervention.

But in a so-called normal life there was often little incentive to think about meaning. And survivors of trauma had little choice. They had to find meaning through suffering or give in to despair and let it destroy their identities, humanity, and dignity. They could survive only by embracing a larger sense of purpose that might not always explain the suffering, but could encompass and transcend it.

Meaning, Frankl believed, could be found in life even when one confronted a hopeless situation—even when facing a fate that could not be changed.

According to Frankl's therapeutic approach, called logotherapy, people could discover meaning in life in three different ways: by creating a work or doing a deed, by experiencing something or encountering someone, and by the attitude they take toward unavoidable suffering. People might find meaning by experiencing goodness, truth, and beauty—for example, in the natural world. Or they could find meaning by experiencing and loving another human being.

And a good sign that people were healing, Frankl found, was a desire to engage in meaningful work.

In her subtle way, Mary Fabri had been encouraging him to find his own purpose, and after four years of working with her, he finally found his bearings. He wanted to be a psychiatrist. He had seen too much blood and dying in the camps, and he did not want to sew up another wound. He had liked talking to fellow prisoners late at night in the camps, when they would open up about their fears. He wanted to offer words of hope that did not deny the grim reality that surrounded them.

The need for psychiatrists trained in trauma was great, he knew, both in the United States and in countries in which entire populations were grappling with the aftermath of terror.

Early on, he thought he would be a stellar psychiatrist simply because he had survived. But he learned from Fabri that a person does not have to survive extreme trauma to be a good therapist. The patient is the ultimate teacher about trauma, and a good therapist is a good listener.

He knew what he was up against. Many psychiatrists and psychologists he had encountered did not think he should be treating other survivors. They seemed to feel that survivors were too fragile to hear stories of horror, or perhaps they pictured them overwhelming patients with the details of their own stories. But during his four years counseling patients he had rarely mentioned his own ordeal. The only evidence of his trauma was in the comments he made to patients to show he believed them.

He felt strongly that psychiatrists who knew little about trauma and attempted to help survivors were a dangerous breed, like the doctors who treated posttraumatic stress disorder only with pills, as if memories of torture could be erased with Valium. More common were the doctors who tried to sidestep the issue of trauma altogether. He once overheard a patient telling a doctor she had been raped by her father. The doctor immediately asked if she was hearing voices. It was easier to talk about hallucinations than to talk about rape, or the aftermath of Katrina, or the war in Iraq. It was easier to talk about immediate effects than to raise hard questions about the nature of evil, the pain of loss, and the challenge of survival.

Who better than a survivor, he thought, to challenge the assumptions about survivors and the best ways to treat them? There was nothing wrong with traumatized people, Boškailo believed. What was wrong was what happened to them. And he questioned the assumption that success could be measured by a decrease in the number of symptoms, rather than by more profound changes in a person's worldview.

It was no longer enough to record tales of atrocities, to count nightmares, and to prescribe pills. "I was convinced that survivors needed to address the kind of questions of meaning raised by Frankl," Boškailo said. "They needed a reason to live, and I wanted to help them find that reason."

Part II

CHAPTER 11
You've Listened to My Words

You've listened to my words
I've told you all I know
—Mak Dizdar

"I am lying down and you are analyzing me," Boškailo told me over the telephone. "I tell you more than anyone in my life."

In the background I could hear Aiša shouting, "You know my husband better than I do!"

It was not true, but sometimes it felt as if I were the keeper of his secrets, the tales with which he did not want to burden Aiša or his sons.

Boškailo's symptoms seemed to lessen after he finished telling me his story. He said he had experienced some relief and a new clarity about what had happened to him. He was his own best evidence of the healing power of storytelling.

I thought I too had held up well, but Boškailo told me otherwise.

"You have secondary trauma, Julia," he said.

"No I don't," I protested. I had no flashbacks or any other major problems. But I did find myself getting stuck on details that would not let go: the man who tried to bite himself to death in the night, the guards who groomed a mentally ill man to be a murderer. I had to confess that at times I was overwhelmed with a sense of hopelessness. I suffered from a low-grade *something*, but I did not know what it was.

"You have secondary trauma," Boškailo repeated. That was the downside, I guess, of being the repository for all things terrible.

Help came during Part II of this book, if only because we lightened up. Our working relationship changed. We cancelled fewer interviews now that Boškailo was no longer having to relive the war. And I did not have to rephrase questions in the hope that Boškailo would talk more about suffering.

In Part I, he had been a witness.

In Part II, he was a healer. And it is a lot easier to talk about hope.

Boškailo was noticeably brighter when he discussed his cases, not because they all had happy endings but because they represented possibility, the chance for patients to get back some of what they had lost.

Aiša, too, changed in Part II of the book. The truth is she had never wanted Esad to do this project. She liked fiction and immersing herself in stories of happier times. It was hard enough for her to endure her own migraines. It was even tougher to see her husband distressed after recalling the past. Enough, she seemed to say. She had a family, a wonderful husband, two beautiful sons. Why go crawling back to the camps?

Boškailo told me later that when he asked Aiša how he could handle more of my questions, she showed little sympathy.

"You wanted to do a book," she told him. "Do a book."

So I was taken aback one day when Aiša's best friend, Zina, called to invite me to be the surprise guest at Aiša and Esad's anniversary party. The family had moved to Phoenix in the summer of 1999 when Esad began a residency program at Maricopa Integrated Health Systems, where he would later work as an attending physician.

I flew to Phoenix the day before the festivities to hang out with Zina in her bright, spacious home filled with flowers.

The next day dozens of guests—men in pants and casual, loose shirts, women in summer dresses, and children in party clothes—arrived by the hour at Zina's backyard patio.

The guests were carrying platters of Bosnian food: pita, ćevapi (small grilled sausages of lamb and beef), sogan dolma (onions stuffed with minced meat), filovane paprika, fried bell peppers, and plates of baklava and other European sweets to complement the feast Zina had already set out.

It struck me as the happiest gathering I had ever seen of a group of Bosnians, but I couldn't help looking at the faces of the older men and women and wondering where they had been.

Aiša looked delighted when I popped out from behind a wall like a minor celebrity. Boškailo wiped a few tears from his eyes.

I gave a little speech, though I do not remember what I said, except that I mentioned how Boškailo described to me the first time he saw Aiša: "She was just beautiful for me. Oh my God."

Boškailo was delighted to hear his words.

"You are now our friend," he said.

Years ago, a writer friend told me that she would never see a therapist who had survived a concentration camp, because her problems would seem too small in comparison.

Diana Ortiz, a nun I interviewed who had survived torture in Guatemala, told me that the unwillingness of people to talk about problems in front of her only made her feel more alone.

Jonathan Shay, the psychiatrist who wrote *Achilles in Vietnam: Combat Trauma and the Undoing of Character*, warns against hierarchies of suffering and writes that no one's suffering can be measured against another's.

Still, I shared my friend's belief. The vicissitudes of everyday life did not compare to life in the camps.

Then my mother died and my marriage ended in divorce, and I was spending my days mourning and my nights writing a book about loss.

Aiša wanted to talk about my situation. I do not think Boškailo said more than that he was very sorry. But soon he added the end of a marriage to the litany of traumas we discussed each day.

"When a person is confined to a concentration camp or loses a parent or goes through the trauma of divorce . . . ," he would say.

It was my loss and he understood.

CHAPTER 12
Only Remembering

And it goes on being stormy outside and the evening
Goes on just as the life goes on which
No I don't seem to be living only remembering
—Abdulah Sidran

A poster of an early Salvador Dalí painting, *Figure at a Window*, hung on the wall of Boškailo's office, a sunny room furnished with three comfortable leather chairs. His staff members at the trauma clinic did not like the blue and lavender scene of a woman looking onto a bay. They would have preferred bright flowers to cheer up the patients. But Boškailo found the picture dreamlike and soothing.

If anyone needed soothing it was his patient Kamil. At their first session, Kamil arrived early and began talking before he sat down. Boškailo was used to taciturn patients who dreaded their first encounter with a psychiatrist. Kamil seemed to have anticipated this meeting for years.

Kamil was a veteran who had fought for the Iraqi army when it invaded Iran in 1980. It had been twenty-five years since he was on the front line. Now he was about Boškailo's age, fifty, and too portly to fit into his old military uniform.

Boškailo was aided by Tima, a petite interpreter who had worked as a pediatrician in Iraq. Tima managed to convey warmth without being intrusive, by leaning toward patients when she asked for clarification and laughing softly at their jokes. She had proved invaluable in the past, not just for translating patients' words, but for giving Boškailo cultural cues about everything from religious dietary restrictions to cultural attitudes about shame.

Clinicians often rely on family members as young as ten years old to translate for traumatized patients, either because the hospital will not pay for an interpreter or because the therapist assumes an interpreter will be a distraction. But a father is not going to discuss killing in front of a child, and a mother is not going to talk about being raped. Many patients do not mind the presence of interpreters who are not from their home countries. Kamil would only allow another Iraqi to speak for him. Kamil had come to the United States to live with his brother three years earlier and had been admitted to a psychiatric hospital just days after his arrival. He had become hysterical soon after arriving in his new home, flailing his arms, stamping his feet, and threatening to kill himself. He needed a doctor, he told his brother. He needed a hospital. It was as if he were more comfortable in a hospital bed than in his own. From then on he was shuttled between hospitals and his brother's apartment.

A doctor who had heard about Boškailo's work with trauma patients sent Kamil to the clinic.

"They sent me to you because you're an expert," Kamil told Boškailo. "You're a real American doctor."

Kamil smiled broadly. Tima and Boškailo smiled, too. Boškailo did not bother to correct him. Kamil wanted an expert, an American expert, the top man in the field to take his case.

Boškailo was struck by how warm and charming Kamil was despite his pain. And Boškailo hoped he could be the "expert" who brought him some solace.

While his other patients often took weeks, months, or years to tell their stories, Kamil wanted Boškailo to have all the details right away. So he described a battlefield in Iraq in 1985.

Kamil spoke slowly, with an intensity of emotion, as if he were narrating a film. He was with a team of soldiers defending their position when he saw the Iranian tanks coming. The Iraqi soldiers were running every which way to avoid the oncoming vehicles. But they were moving too quickly. Kamil took off to the right. But even running at top speed, he could hear the tanks rolling over the bodies of friends who had run in other directions. The smell was intense.

"I could not breathe," Kamil told Boškailo. "And ever since

then I cannot stop focusing on my breathing. In and out. In and out. In and out. It's all I can do. Breathe in and out. I can't do anything else."

He cried easily, he told Boškailo, and every evening he had nightmares. Sometimes he had panic attacks, and he was too anxious to leave the house. His suicidal threats landed him in the hospital.

"Oh my God," said Boškailo, overwhelmed by the thought of a man monitoring his breath for decades. "It's unbelievable. It must be difficult to even talk about."

He had long ago stopped thinking in advance about something meaningful to say after a story of terror. He figured patients preferred a genuine response, even an awkward one, to a statement about suffering that was clearly rehearsed.

Survivors have different ways of coming to terms with their histories. Boškailo's wife, Aiša, told him that for years she walked around writing a novel in her head about her experiences during the war, and she did not feel better until she had "written" the last chapter. Other survivors write testimonials for future generations.

Some find so much comfort in talking to fellow survivors, they never need to share their experiences in a psychiatrist's office. But most people, Boškailo believed, need to say aloud what happened, to begin to understand the trauma they endured, to feel a sense of relief and a lessening of overpowering negative emotions. They begin to become aware of their own resiliency when they hear themselves describing the horror they survived.

Boškailo always reminded patients that they were in control of how much to tell about their experiences and when. Telling the story in a place they consider safe to a person they see as compassionate can lessen the hold a traumatic experience has on them. The experience is about being heard and grappling with the feelings that arise. In the best cases, Boškailo believed survivors experienced feelings contrary to those they had felt during their trauma. They had been denied safety. Now they felt safe. They had been threatened. Now they felt supported.

The psychiatrist Richard Mollica calls the process "the biological miracle of empathy," a phrase Boškailo felt captured the interaction between doctor and patient. Mollica's research has concluded that storytelling can elicit rational thoughts about a traumatic situation "while simultaneously sidestepping the stimulation of strong emotions." The result is the reduction of emotional memories that no longer help patients cope.

The job of a therapist, Boškailo believed, was also learning what was important to a patient, be it people, experiences, or objects. Boškailo had a T-shirt he treasured that had been signed by every prisoner in Ljubuški. One day he found it in the garbage. He couldn't believe it. Aiša had thrown it out.

"In the garbage!" he said to her. "My Ljubuški shirt in the garbage!"

Aiša was genuinely surprised at his attachment to the old shirt.

"I never saw you wear it," she said.

Kamil was comforted telling his story to a willing listener who appreciated the gravity of his experience. Indeed, the story seemed to lessen its hold on him.

Just knowing that Boškailo could handle hearing how his comrades died clearly led Kamil to feel more secure during their weekly sessions. Boškailo talked to him about the normal feelings of survivors' guilt experienced by many who lost people in combat or natural disasters, and reminded him that he was not responsible for the surprise attack. Boškailo was not sure that Kamil had taken in fully what he had to say, and he returned to this message again and again.

Boškailo agreed with Viktor Frankl, who said that the quality of the relationship mattered more than any one therapeutic technique. Frankl once described listening to a suicidal patient and then talking to her for half an hour. Afterward, it was humbling for Frankl to realize that she had barely listened to his words of wisdom. She was impressed instead that Frankl had taken the time to listen to her troubles. She decided that a world in which someone would listen to her was a world worth living in.

Kamil decided that it was worth telling his story because he was beginning to feel better and was relieved that he would never have to tell it again. "I already told you my story," he would say. And one time for Kamil was enough.

————

Boškailo was not the first doctor to note that Kamil suffered from posttraumatic stress disorder (PTSD), defined by the American Psychiatric Association as the development of symptoms following a psychologically distressing event that is outside the range of normal human experience. "The person's response to the event must involve intense fear, helplessness or horror," the association notes.

Although the diagnosis was not added to the manual for treating psychiatric disorders until 1980, the condition has been observed for many years. During the American Civil War, the men who showed the most visible signs of distress after trauma were said to be suffering from "nostalgia," as if they were longing for better days. During World War I, the condition was known as "shell shock." Later, it was called "combat exhaustion."

Survivors of the Holocaust rarely sought treatment for trauma, the most obvious reason being that little was available. According to the psychiatrist Paul Chodoff, West German authorities refused to provide money for survivors' psychotherapy, and some worried that they would not receive reparations if they sought treatment. Furthermore, they did not want to be considered "mental patients" rather than reliable witnesses to unspeakable crimes.

The most common traumas occur during a serious threat to one's life or that of close relatives and friends, or during the sudden destruction of one's home or community. PTSD can also result after one has seen another person subjected to extreme violence or seen a survivor of such an attack. Classic symptoms of PTSD include outbursts of anger, problems concentrating, chronic fatigue, hyperarousal (such as a heightened startle response), and high-risk behavior (such as drug abuse). Survivors may avoid places or situations that bring to mind the trauma and may become psychologically numb and unable to experience joy.

The psychiatrist Frank Ochberg, editor of the first text on the treatment of PTSD, says it should only be diagnosed "when an event of major dimension—a searing, stunning, haunting event—has clearly occurred and is relived, despite strenuous attempts to avoid the memory."

The lifetime prevalence of PTSD is 10.4 percent among women and 5 percent among men. And many patients with PTSD have at least one other disorder, such as depression. The higher incidence among women, according to a review of twenty-five years of research by the International Society of Traumatic Stress Studies (ISTSS), may be attributed to the fact that women are more likely than men to have experienced sexual assault and childhood sexual abuse, which are more likely to result in PTSD than other forms of trauma. According to a study published by the Rand Center for Military Health Policy Research, *The Invisible Wounds of War*, upward of 26 percent of returning troops from Iraq and Afghanistan may have mental health conditions, PTSD being the most common.

The results of controlled trials cited by the International Society for Traumatic Stress Studies have shown that attempts by professionals to treat survivors of trauma during or immediately after the event do not prevent the onset of PTSD. In addition, PTSD should not be diagnosed until symptoms have lasted at least one month, to ensure that the reaction is not a temporary response to a crisis. It must be noted, however, that survivors who do not meet the criteria for PTSD often suffer greatly and need to make sense of their experience and integrate it into their lives.

Some professionals reject the PTSD diagnosis altogether. In his book *Post-Traumatic Stress Disorder: Malady or Myth?*, the psychologist Chris Brewin describes a "long drawn-out struggle" between advocates and skeptics. Since the diagnosis was introduced in 1980, he writes, influential opinion makers have questioned the "legitimacy of the diagnosis and the very existence of supposedly traumatic reactions." So-called PTSD symptoms, they say, are rarely seen in non-Western countries. Even seriously depressed people, they argue, will recover naturally over time, and widespread PTSD counseling creates a culture of victims.

Brewin is among those specialists who note that flashbacks do not occur a few months after a traumatic incident in people who do not have PTSD. While some people recover naturally within a few months, a subgroup will continue to have serious symptoms and will be at risk of developing long-term problems if they do not receive treatment. And such symptoms are consistent across cultures, not just in the West.

The International Society of Traumatic Stress Studies calls PTSD an extensively investigated and well-validated disorder. Furthermore, according to the ISTSS, the use of rigorous scientific methods to assess the efficacy of treatment has increased dramatically in the past twenty-five years.

Most therapists specializing in trauma today espouse a bio-psycho-social model that pairs psychotherapy with drugs, including selective serotonin reuptake inhibitors and other antidepressants that have proved helpful in relieving the symptoms of PTSD. Sleeping medication may also be needed to end chronic insomnia, which can exacerbate depression. In addition, this model calls for doctors to address patients' social needs, such as housing and employment, acknowledging that in some cases a job can do as much for a patient's psyche as an antidepressant.

No one treatment works for all patients, and Boškailo agrees with Mary Fabri that the patient should guide the healer on how they can best work together. Boškailo and his colleagues in Chicago and Phoenix practice several types of psychotherapy combined with medication and screening for drug and alcohol addiction. Cognitive therapy, which is usually short term, helps patients recognize and challenge distortions in thinking that lead to depression. The ISTSS has found evidence that cognitive therapy is effective in treating PTSD "quite compelling." Boškailo also opts for long-term psychotherapy, which helps his most severely traumatized patients acknowledge their losses; foster resiliency, the capacity to mobilize their coping resources; and find meaning that can help them thrive.

Another method shown to be valuable for survivors of trauma is eye movement desensitization and reprocessing (EMDR). Therapists guide patients through bilateral eye movements, as part of a program designed to enhance the processing of traumatic memories. Once considered hocus-pocus by many professionals, EMDR is now widely accepted by the ISTSS and others. Some patients also respond well to yoga, meditation, and spiritual practices that emphasize growth after trauma.

Boškailo admires psychiatrists who work in countries that have been devastated by war and natural disaster, such as Iraq and Rwanda. In Bosnia, Mollica has provided comprehensive mental-health training—with an emphasis on the power of storytelling—to Bosnian primary-health colleagues so they can treat tens of thousands of people. In 1999, the psychologist Jack Saul founded Refuge, a community-based program for survivors of torture and refugee trauma. Following the attacks on the World Trade Center in 2001, Refuge established the Downtown Community Resource Center, a psychosocial program for residents and workers.

———

Kamil could have been living anywhere, Boškailo thought, because he felt at home nowhere. In Iraq, he had witnessed the killing of friends who had become a second family. Then, not long after the war, Kamil's wife divorced the husband she could no longer recognize. He also lost the family members he depended on for company and support. His father and all of his brothers and sisters left Iraq to come to the United States as soon as they could. Kamil stayed behind with his mother, just the two of them in a cramped apartment, breathing in and out all through the day.

He sought psychiatric care in Iraq, and he tried vial after vial of antidepressants and anti-anxiety pills. Nothing helped, he told Boškailo. The doctors had gotten it wrong. After his mother died, he went all the way to Syria to see a doctor who specialized in treating traumatized patients. He got a different medication, and then another, to no avail.

"But you can help me," he told Boškailo. "American doctors. You know everything!"

Kamil grew increasingly attached to his doctor. One week he was so full of enthusiasm he raced up to Boškailo and kissed him on the forehead and forearm. Confused, Boškailo turned to Tima, who told him in English that such effusiveness was a way of showing respect.

Boškailo endured two more weeks of kisses before he felt comfortable explaining that American doctors preferred handshakes. After that Kamil began every session with an energetic handshake, as if to let Boškailo know he was embracing this new tradition.

Boškailo learned that Kamil was a very religious man, an Orthodox Christian who went to church regularly and prayed often for comfort. ("God comes first, then Dr. Boškailo," he'd say.) Boškailo knew that Kamil's faith could be a source of strength if he could just get beyond his fixation with pills.

Kamil's initial exuberance did not last. He skipped the usual handshake the next time he arrived at Boškailo's office. And he seemed resigned to another round of useless therapy in a foreign country.

"You're not helping me," he said to Boškailo.

Boškailo was having the same concerns. Kamil was getting better in that most nights he was sleeping with the help of medication, and he had not been hospitalized since starting therapy. But Boškailo had not been able to convince him that he needed to acknowledge the magnitude of his losses and take some responsibility for his own healing, rather than relying on some easy fix. And he was still fixating on his breathing.

"You don't believe I can help you," Boškailo told Kamil. "You only have faith in pills."

"What about ECT?" Kamil asked, meaning electroshock (or electroconvulsive) therapy. He had heard about ECT from the doctor in Syria.

"I do not treat people with trauma with ECT," Boškailo said.

"You need to read more. You need to study more," Kamil said. "You need to find the right medicine. Have you consulted your supervisors about me?"

"Yes, I have talked to my colleagues about you. And you are welcome to get a second opinion."

"Ask them to help you," Kamil urged. "Ask them about medicine."

Boškailo had believed that he could do more than the other doctors who had failed Kamil, but maybe that was just his vanity. Perhaps Kamil would never find solace in a therapist's office. Perhaps he was as well as he was ever going to be. It was a depressing thought.

When Kamil arrived for the next session, he found Boškailo taping a piece of white poster board to an easel in the middle of the room. In the center of the board he drew a circle. Inside he drew a large stick figure. "What are you doing?" Kamil asked the doctor.

"This is you," he told Kamil, pointing at the stick figure.

Kamil sat down in the leather chair, his eyes fixated on the primitive drawing.

Then Boškailo divided the circle into eight triangles. In the first triangle he wrote the word wife.

In the second, mother.

In the third, friends.

In the fourth, cousins.

In the fifth, home.

In the sixth, job.

In the seventh, country.

In the eighth, culture.

Then one by one Boškailo crossed out the words in the triangles.

"Kamil, you don't have your wife, your mother, your friends, your cousins, your home, your job, your country, your culture, your television, your books."

Kamil began to cry, then he got up and began pounding on Boškailo's desk with his fists.

"I can't stand it. I need pills!" he pleaded.

"I have no pill to take away loss."

Boškailo had heard of similar losses from American soldiers suffering from PTSD. They had returned to the United States only to find their environment completely changed. They no longer had their jobs. Friends had gone off to marry and have children. Now they carried the identity of soldier, killer, and survivor. Jonathan Shay was correct when he wrote, "Our culture has been notably deficient in providing for reception of the Furies of War into community." Boškailo often thought the U.S. Department of Veterans

Affairs would be wise to focus on building communities for returning soldiers who had no place to call home.

Boškailo had been hoping that his sketch would make concrete a pain Kamil could not yet articulate, and the drawing seemed to have an even more dramatic effect than Boškailo had anticipated.

In the upcoming weeks, Kamil began to acknowledge that his wife was not coming back, his mother was not coming back, and he was not going home to Iraq anytime soon.

"Is there a pill that can replace all of this, Kamil?"

"No," he said.

But the realization that no pill would take away his loss left Kamil bereft. If there was no pill, there was no hope.

"So I will always be sick," he told Boškailo.

"No, you won't," Boškailo replied. "After what happened to you, you are a different person. You will always have this memory, but it will be less disturbing. You have lost a lot, but you can replace some of these things, with a new culture, a new language. You can begin filling in the circle."

Kamil seemed moved by the gravity of the statement, and he liked the idea of filling in the circle with the doctor's help.

Boškailo believed that it was the therapist's job to help survivors of trauma regain some of the things they had lost, and he was determined to help Kamil begin again. He and Fabri agreed that therapists need to be social workers or a liaison to social workers at community agencies. And it was helpful to maintain ties with community leaders, cultural and religious leaders, and local businesses that could provide jobs.

A colleague had asked him if he was afraid of losing his professional boundaries. He had strong internal boundaries, Boškailo said, and he was careful not to give patients the impression that he would rescue them. But if he had kept the rigid boundaries he had been taught in medical school, patients like Kamil would be lost.

First, Kamil needed help with housing. He hated living an isolated life under the critical eye of his brother, so Boškailo arranged for him to live in a residential center for people with mental illness, and to be transported to the local Orthodox church.

For the first time, Kamil used the charm he had turned on

with Boškailo to make new friends in both the church and the residential center. Nothing encouraged Boškailo more than hearing stories of Kamil's friends, with their various eccentricities and infirmities. The man who had spent his days and nights alone in his brother's home was finally branching out.

Kamil was more ready to consider remedies that did not come in a bottle. Still, sometimes he would jump out of his chair and scream at Boškailo.

"You have to help me! How come I am not better?"

"You are fifty, not twenty-five. You will never be the person you were twenty-five years ago. Even if you didn't have trauma you would not be the same."

So, again, they returned to what Kamil had lost, and again they talked about how to regain some of those losses and to find a sense of purpose in his new life. And it struck Boškailo again how much courage it took for a man who had lost so much to begin all over.

During almost every session they discussed his future, because traumatized people often have trouble envisioning a future.

"Tell me about your plans, Kamil. What are you going to do?"

Initially, Kamil told Boškailo simply that he wanted to cultivate a better relationship with his father and brother and to improve his English. After years in and out of hospitals he hoped to be independent and productive. That was his purpose.

"I want to be a man," he told Boškailo. "A man has a wife and job and a house and money."

Later, as he learned some English, Kamil would try out his new vocabulary on Boškailo.

"You are beautiful, doctor," Kamil told him.

"You think I'm beautiful?" Boškailo said.

Kamil blushed. He had meant to say "good."

"What would you like to do now?" Boškailo asked Kamil.

"Work," Kamil said. He did not have any money. He wanted his own money.

So he started seeing a social worker, who helped him find a menial job packing boxes in a factory. He had worked as an auto mechanic in Iraq, but now he was happy just to be employed. When he got his first paycheck, he brought a picture of a watch in *Esquire* magazine to his therapy session.

"How much does this cost?"

"About twenty thousand dollars," Boškailo told him. "But I saw a watch for twenty dollars at TJ Maxx."

"It was a big deal for him to have a good watch," Boškailo recalled. "A man is not a man without a good watch. Next came the gold chain, and he was really happy."

At their weekly sessions, Boškailo reviewed Kamil's progress. He had a new home, a job, new friends, a television, some books. Most important, during working hours his mind was so occupied he forgot about monitoring his breath.

He had not talked much about the wife who left him, but now he was dreaming of marrying again. "Tell me when I am healthy so I can get married. I don't want to get married if I'm sick."

Boškailo would have liked to see Kamil live on his own in an apartment, find a job as a mechanic, maybe date a nice Iraqi woman.

"I would have liked to help him more," Boškailo said.

But he reminded himself that a fifty-year-old man was not a twenty-five-year-old man. A veteran was no longer listening to himself breathe in and out. And there was no pill to take away loss.

CHAPTER 13

An Island in the Heart of the World

I am an island
In the heart of the world and nothing
Reaches me. Nothing but the torpid
Blood and the shudder going through it.
A silence, surrounded by nothing.
—Abdulah Sidran

His patient Emir was a little old for the black curly hair that brushed his shoulders. He was about forty, Boškailo guessed, handsome with a strong chin and chiseled features. After the war with Serbia he and his wife found refuge in Germany, where they had lived for a dozen years. Before that he was an importer in northern Bosnia who traveled often to Italy and Turkey to buy fancy clothes, which he sold on the black market back home.

Boškailo figured that Emir must have been charismatic in his day. He pictured him in Italian suits selling silk shirts to fashionable Bosnians and bantering with them about the news of the day. But he had to be tough to make it on the black market, and tough guys were not always keen on therapy.

He sat stiffly in his chair, as if he had not decided whether to go or stay.

"So why are you here?" Boškailo asked him.

Emir shrugged. But after a few minutes of uncomfortable silence, he decided to fill Boškailo in on the bare bones of his story.

Boškailo never pushed patients to tell their story. Fabri had let him reveal his own tale slowly, week after week. He believed

101

that survivors who had been denied control should be allowed to shape their own histories, telling as much or as little as they liked in their own time. Learning to make sense of what happened to them did not always require a complete accounting or a beginning, middle, and end. Some patients never told their whole story and still experienced the therapeutic benefit that could come from disclosure.

Forcing patients to tell their stories when they did not feel safe could be very damaging, he believed, especially in a public setting. The television reporter who wanted a quick recap of a horrific event from a survivor in front of a camera could end up retraumatizing that person, resulting in an increase of symptoms such as flashbacks and nightmares.

But like Kamil, Emir was eager to tell his story, if only to get it over with, and he wanted to tell the whole thing.

Before the war, he told Boškailo, most of his friends had been Serbian and, given that he was not a religious man, Emir had considered himself Yugoslav, not Muslim. Boškailo understood his connection to the Serbs. Boškailo's best man had been Serbian, and in Bosnia a best man was a brother for life. But Emir was unusual in that he had blended in seamlessly with the Serbian community.

He had even married a Serbian woman, whom he considered the love of his life.

"We were all the same," he told Boškailo, his voice cracking before he regained his composure.

Then came the war with the Serbs. One afternoon armed Serbian guards went from house to house in Emir's town and ordered entire families to follow them to a soccer field. Emir recognized one of the guards, an acquaintance from grade school. But the blank look on his face told Emir that greetings would be futile. The guards escorted him and his wife to the soccer field, where they took their place on the cement next to friends and neighbors, who looked more puzzled than fearful. The few people who had thought to bring bread shared it with the others, and they assumed they would be let go within hours. After all, they were guilty of nothing.

They were standing for hours when the guards walked through the crowd ordering the women and children to board army trucks. Emir held onto his wife's hand as she was dragged away by a guard who looked too young to shave. He thought she looked terrified. Emir felt sick trying to imagine where they were taking his wife and overwhelmed by the senselessness of it all. He later learned that the Serbs had driven the women and children to the Serbian border, where they let them go without food or money.

The men talked about the possibilities for themselves. They could be kicked out of Bosnia. They could be shot. Then the guards announced that all the men over eighteen would be boarding buses. They left a few old men to fend for themselves.

As they stood on the bus, knocking into each other when the driver raced over potholes, the men looked at their surroundings to see if they could recognize landmarks. Emir's group was taken up north, where they were unloaded onto the grounds of a former school building that once housed Serb, Croatian, and Bosniak children.

Classrooms became holding cells filled with men standing shoulder to shoulder. Offices were used for solitary confinement.

Emir spent most of this time in solitary, though he had no idea why he was singled out for the honor. The days were boring, the nights were hell. Guards kicked him in the torso with boots, breaking three ribs, and bashed his head against the wall. They wanted information, but Emir had nothing to tell them. He was a black-market salesman, not a politician or intelligence officer. So the beatings continued each night, and each night Emir passed out.

In three months Emir did the unthinkable. Because it was a makeshift camp run by amateurs, he grabbed a piece of wood, stood on a ledge inside the window, and used the wood to make a hole in the wall so he could get access to the attic. He pulled himself up into the attic, jumped off the roof, and ran. He kept running until he made it the Sava River, which formed the northern border of Bosnia, with the Croatian territory on the north bank. Within a week he crossed into Germany.

"Do you believe me?" Emir asked Boškailo.

"Of course," Boškailo said.

As a therapist, Boškailo believed that the patient's feelings while telling a story mattered more than the details. Memory was not always reliable in the healthiest of patients who had witnessed a crime, and traumatized patients sometimes had difficulty recollecting each event exactly as it happened. Still, lawyers for perpetrators often claimed that survivors who had indeed suffered traumatic experiences could not be relied on if there was the slightest discrepancy in their stories or if they had experienced flashbacks. Such lawyers were penalizing survivors for exhibiting the very symptoms that proved they had suffered. In such cases, Boškailo knew, corroborating witnesses and forensic evidence were particularly critical.

If a patient told him a story that was completely implausible, Boškailo would gently question that person on details he was "curious about." But during his career he heard very little distortion of major events, even in the cases of patients forced to eat human flesh.

And in Emir's case Boškailo had been told of his river crossing by members of the Bosnian community. Boškailo had also heard that Emir and his wife had been reunited in Germany.

Ultimately, it was Boškailo's job to let patients know they had been heard.

Both he and Fabri felt that their job was to be witnesses. They needed to acknowledge the political reality of the time, the people who had died, and those who had survived atrocities. It would be wrong, he believed, not to say he knew which political leaders, soldiers, and common citizens had committed verifiable acts of aggression.

The psychiatrist Robert Jay Lifton said his work in Hiroshima convinced him that it was immoral to claim "professional neutrality" in the face of such destruction. And when he and Boškailo were introduced at a conference on trauma, Lifton said, "I hope you are using your own experience in helping survivors."

The psychiatrist Jonathan Shay wrote that he had been politicized by his work and now saw that treatment must be morally engaged—that trauma work can never be apolitical, that an affectively neutral position will defeat healing.

The psychiatrist Judith Herman agreed: "It is morally impossible to remain neutral in this conflict. The bystander is forced to takes sides." There was no room for neutrality when patients bore the scars of grave human-rights abuses.

———————

When he arrived at Boškailo's office now, Emir let his body sink into the soft leather chair. He was a little less anxious, and he opened up enough to talk about his physical pain.

"I have nightmares and my whole body aches," Emir told Boškailo. "I feel worse now than I did back then. What can you do for me?"

"I can't take away what happened," Boškailo told him. But he could help him imagine a better future.

Such assurances did little to lessen Emir's irritability. He had no interest in talking about the future or even the present. Boškailo doubted that he had ever spoken about his feelings to anyone but his wife. He remained fixated on the betrayal, and Boškailo wondered if he could get past the image of friends turning on friends.

During every session Emir unleashed his anger at his Serbian neighbors, who, he said, betrayed friends who had shown them nothing but loyalty. He was always the hero in these long-running narratives. And he talked about his regrets. He was mad at himself for having left Germany—or rather for letting Germany expel him and his wife along with thousands of Bosnian refugees. If he had not been married, he told himself, he could have gone into hiding. Now he was in a new country, and he did not know a word of the language and could no longer work.

What he did not talk about, Boškailo noticed, were the feelings behind the anger. He never mentioned missing one of his friends. He never talked about his evenings at café bars being replaced by lonely nights. Once again, Boškailo was convinced that patients had to acknowledge their losses before they could move on with their lives.

So the next time Emir talked about betrayals, Boškailo brought up the subject of loss. Given Emir's degree of resistance, Boškailo did not worry about being heavy handed.

"Before the war I would have died for the guys who kicked me in the head," Emir told him.

"So you lost the Serbian people?" Boškailo said.

"Fuck you," Emir replied.

"You lost your friends."

Silence.

"You lost your evenings in the café bar. You lost your work. You lost your language."

"Shut the fuck up."

Emir's outburst sounded more fearful than mad, and Boškailo did not think he was a violent man. Finally, Emir sat back in his chair and spent the rest of the session in silence. Boškailo wondered whether Emir had taken in his words or just repelled them in a rage. Would therapy continue to be a recounting of past injustices, or was Emir capable of imagining a future?

———

At the start of the next session, Emir surprised the doctor by thanking him. Emir did not say why he was thankful. But Boškailo knew instinctively that Emir was grateful someone had acknowledged his losses.

For the first time in his therapy, Emir revealed a little less anger and a hint of vulnerability. He had been hurt by the friends who left him, he said. And he was less concerned about cataloging the injustices than with understanding the roots.

"Why did they turn on me?" Emir asked Boškailo.

"I wish I knew," Boškailo answered.

He had heard this question again and again. His patients wanted to know the reason for their suffering and how human beings could behave so cruelly.

Virtually every patient asked him why they had been singled out for such brutal treatment. "What had I done?" they asked. They had done nothing, he assured them. They needed to hear from another person that they had not been responsible. And when they asked again, he reminded them again.

Perhaps if he had been more traditionally religious he would have felt better equipped to offer explanations of why friends turned on friends. Certainly his religious patients seemed to have the easiest time making sense of the terror, and it was important to draw on these beliefs to aid the healing process. The small percentage of Bosnian Muslims who were observant had an extraordinary acceptance of what had happened to them: it was God's will. If they had lost a loved one far too young, God had a reason for taking the person. People were not just dying; they were going to another place.

It was important for Boškailo to appreciate how his patients understood the world in order to help them heal, and that meant learning about ideas that were foreign to him, such as the belief in some cultures that spirit possession can cause psychological illness.

It was also critical for Boškailo to acknowledge those people who had lost their faith given the magnitude of their horror. The psychiatrist Shay wrote, "God's love for humankind is one of our present culture's all-pervasive, invisible, unquestioned, and thus unconscious assumptions. When war shattered this assumption, American soldiers in Vietnam lost a sustaining idea. . . . God has vanished and taken it all with him." Like Shay, Boškailo had to help patients recognize their loss and realize that they could embrace another kind of meaningful narrative that links past, present, and future and acknowledges the tragedy they witnessed.

Many of his patients were "in-betweens." They had faith, but not the kind they could articulate, not the kind that brought them to a mosque or a church for regular prayer. Too many religious leaders had already offered them pat answers about God's will, and many patients refused to discuss religion altogether.

Boškailo agreed with Victor Frankl that man cannot understand the ultimate meaning of human suffering, because ultimately such concerns were matters of believing, not thinking.

What could Boškailo say to Emir? He could talk about nationalism and fundamentalism. But what would he have to say about the nature of evil that philosophers and theologians had not said better?

So he told Emir what he believed deeply: some people had to search for meaning without ever knowing the reason why.

Should survivors forgive their perpetrators? some patients asked him.

He had seen Christian evangelists go to scenes of tragedy and encourage people to forgive. By holding on to anger, the reasoning went, survivors were hindering their own recovery. But Boškailo knew too many survivors who had been made to feel guilty that they could not forgive and forget.

He offered his full support to patients who felt the need to exonerate the guilty. When the power of absolution was central to one's understanding of the world, forgiveness could genuinely lead to a sense of peace.

But for Boškailo such a thought was unfathomable. How could a mother excuse a man who killed her children? He agreed strongly with the concentration camp survivor Elie Wiesel when he said, One cannot forgive on behalf of the dead.

————

Emir had talked about the nightmares that kept him thrashing in bed, but he avoided bringing up his other symptoms. Perhaps Emir thought a man who had escaped a concentration camp should have overcome his fears. But after being in solitary for three months, Emir was afraid to go into enclosed areas and public places. His biggest fear was riding an elevator, lest he have a panic attack.

Boškailo used exposure therapy, in which patients are gently and repeatedly exposed to sights and sounds they fear, to make them less sensitive to such stimuli.

He encouraged Emir to take his nephew to the grocery store and stay there for no more than a minute, almost as if challenging a panic attack to overtake him. "Don't buy anything," Boškailo told him. "Just leave quickly." He asked Emir to return in two hours to the same store, staying a few seconds longer. Then Boškailo asked Emir to go back again, this time for a few minutes.

Emir repeated this exercise for several days in a row.

After the second week, Boškailo told Emir to buy cigarettes or a pack of gum.

Soon Emir was going to the store several times a day. Within two months, he was going by himself.

The next challenge was the elevator. Boškailo asked Emir to accompany him to the elevator across the street from his office, where a crew happened to be filming a movie.

They waited for the elevator, and Boškailo assured Emir that he would be all right.

"There is nothing to be afraid of."

Then the door opened, and standing inside was the actor Bruce Willis.

Willis nodded and said hello. Emir smiled broadly.

Later, Emir told anyone who would listen that he took his first elevator ride in the United States with Bruce Willis.

Boškailo was beginning to think of psychiatric patients in much the same way that a cardiologist looks at his heart patients. When a patient has heart surgery, the only predictive factor for recovery is how much reserve the heart has. Boškailo thought more about the reserve in his patients' hearts. What was their capacity for forming and transforming relationships?

Frankl's logotherapy focused on the future, the meaning that was to be realized by the patient in the coming days. But the key to finding meaning, Boškailo believed, was in the life led before the trauma. What had been his patients' plans, their hopes, their dreams? How would they have described their purpose in life before the trauma? How would they have described their relationships? If Aiša and his sons had taught him anything, it was that relationships were at the heart of finding meaning: connections with spouses, family members, co-workers, neighbors, and the world at large.

When Emir began talking about his life before the trauma, Boškailo knew it was a good sign. He would mention a soccer game from the 1970s or a cup of coffee with friends with a vividness that made Boškailo yearn for a cup himself. He told captivating stories about the crazier Bosnians and Serbs who took up residence at the café bars in Bosnia and their long-winded tales of heroism in war, and Boškailo found himself looking forward to the next tale. For the first time Boškailo noticed a hint of the amiable man who had won over customers with his expensive clothing. There was nothing Boškailo liked better than seeing a person's true self emerge. Small changes, but they let Boškailo know that Emir was no longer stuck in the past.

Finally, Emir addressed the issues that really mattered. He talked about the one Serb who had not betrayed him: his wife. He dreamed about going back to work—for himself, not for some American factory owner. And he planned for the day he would go back to Europe.

But Boškailo sensed that Emir needed more. A man Boškailo might have dismissed earlier as too tough to be reflective was ready to talk about his purpose in life.

All patients, Boškailo believed, needed a life goal, a sense of meaning.

Lifton, who has studied the aftermath of trauma for more than four decades, talks of the quest for authenticity and meaning and the desire of survivors to achieve "symbolic immortality" through work or influence on other human beings, family, spiritual principles, or a psychic state of transcendence.

Herman talks about the importance of a survivor mission and notes that a significant minority of survivors needs to engage in social action, speak out about injustice, and in some cases, confront their perpetrators.

Some of Boškailo's patients found meaning in writing or painting. Others found meaning in rearing and educating their children. Some focused on forming or deepening relationships or finding new work. And some found meaning in recognizing the role they played while they were suffering during the war.

"The way in which a man accepts his fate and all the suffering it entails," Frankl wrote, "the way in which he takes up his cross[,] gives him the opportunity—even under the most difficult circumstances—to add [a] deeper meaning to his life."

Frankl emphasized that a doctor could not tell a patient where meaning lies. But transcriptions of his conversations in *The Will to Meaning: Foundations and Applications of Logotherapy* reveal that Frankl spoke at length to patients about how they suffered bravely and honestly, and he urged them directly to come up with a life goal to find meaning.

Boškailo decided to offer Emir his own thoughts about dignity in the face of war. Like Frankl, he had seen that people can brave the worst conditions—and choose how they respond to those conditions. He never wanted to burden patients with the details of his own experience. But in this case Emir already knew that Boškailo had been in the concentration camps.

He brought up the topic early in a session.

"Sometimes we can reclaim our dignity just by recognizing that we did not fight violence with violence when our friends betrayed us," he told Emir. "If I learned one thing in the camps, it is that we have the ability to choose our attitude and actions in the direst of circumstances.

"Most Bosniaks did not kill any civilians in a war where 200,000 people were killed. What matters is what you did and who you are. That's the only thing you can control."

Emir did not respond right away. But during their next meeting he told Boškailo that he had behaved humanely in inhumane circumstances.

"I didn't kill anyone. I could have killed a guard."

It was then that Boškailo noticed that Emir was beginning to let go of his fixation on betrayal. He had latched onto the idea that he had chosen to behave well under duress, and the macho attitude seemed replaced by a sense of pride.

When Boškailo brought up the subject of finding a new sense of purpose, Emir was ready to consider all the possibilities. He went from being transfixed in the moment to thinking about the future, a sure sign that any trauma patient is well on the road to recovery.

Boškailo would have expected Emir to focus on his work and his desire to support his family, but Emir surprised him by concentrating on the political aftermath of war. Like Herman, Boškailo had discovered that a minority of his patients desperately needed to respond to the political forces that led to terror. For them there was no meaning without justice in the courts. But, like Judith Herman, he had no expectation that his patients would take on a big cause if they were not so inclined.

Emir was so inclined.

He was so proud of not having fought violence with violence that he wanted future generations to know what role each side had played during the war. He felt a new sense of responsibility, which, according to Frankl, went hand in hand with finding meaning that went beyond focusing on himself.

The international tribunal in The Hague had formed, and Emir began reading the Bosnian newspapers and combing the Internet to get the details about the new court. He had hope that the world would know the truth and the guilty would be punished. He had spent months in a camp, but now his guard might spend thirty years in prison.

A man who had resisted telling a doctor his story wanted to testify before the world.

CHAPTER 14
The Heart of This Sadness

We looked
one another in the eyes, summing it up for the thousandth
time. How shall we root out
the heart of this sadness?
—Abdulah Sidran

When forty-five-year-old Emila arrived at Boškailo's office, he thought she looked close to sixty. Hunched over and dressed in a long black skirt like a woman in mourning, she was gaunt and her face looked haggard from months of sleepless nights. She did not make eye contact, and she gripped the arm of her strapping twenty-year-old son.

Boškailo offered them chairs, and the son sat down immediately. Emila stood and began to pace, though the room was much too small for pacing.

Boškailo asked her simple questions.

"How old are you?" Silence.

"What brings you here?" With a nod of her head she signaled to her son to answer while she continued walking back and forth in the cramped space.

When the son mentioned Srebrenica, Boškailo knew what was coming. In the worst massacre in Europe since World War II, Serb soldiers had killed eight thousand civilians over the course of several days in 1995. More than five thousand people had been identified using DNA evidence and other methods, most of them from mass graves discovered eighteen miles north of Srebrenica. Some three thousand victims were buried at the public cemetery. Every year thousands of Bosnians trek to Srebrenica to honor the dead.

"We lost everyone," the son told Boškailo. "We lost my father, my grandfather, my great uncle, and my aunt—so many people I cannot count."

And his mother, Boškailo knew, was not able to bury those she loved.

"She's not eating, and she's not sleeping. She cries all day long," he told Boškailo. She had flashbacks of people being killed in front of her, and some nights she woke up screaming.

Emila continued pacing as if she had not heard her son talking. She had the blank stare of a dead person, and Boškailo could not help wondering whether he would be able help her.

"I will do whatever I can to help," he told them.

It was a mystery why some people responded to tragedy more strongly than others, and Emila had one of the most severe cases of PTSD he had witnessed.

According to Frank Ochberg, there are several possible explanations for why people exposed to the same trauma respond differently. More research needs to be done on the subject. One theory is that minor trauma resolved early in life acts as an "inoculation," creating immunity against major trauma that occurs later. But some studies show that exposure to trauma in childhood, such as sexual abuse, can make people more vulnerable to PTSD. Recent studies of Gulf War veterans, for example, suggest a link between abuse during childhood and combat-related PTSD.

Many, perhaps most, people with PTSD and related conditions are never diagnosed. For clinicians who have not been trained in trauma, it can be uncomfortable to talk about horrific events. At the same time many patients fear they will be labeled crazy if they admit that they are waking up screaming, so they never tell anyone. Boškailo called it double avoidance by therapist and patients.

He was grateful that Emila's son was wise enough to seek help for his mother, though he wished she had come in much sooner. Boškailo prescribed Emila an antidepressant and medication for sleep and asked them both to come back the following week.

Traditionally patients come to their therapist's office alone or are accompanied only by interpreters. But this son was her voice and her lifeline. Without him, she would not come, let alone talk.

Boškailo was aware that some women might be fearful of him just because of his build, and they might be better off seeing another therapist. Most Serbs who raped Bosnian women were tall, bearded men—and he was a tall, bearded man. But he found that even women who had endured the worst kind of degradation at the hands of men were able to trust him when they sensed he understood what they had lost.

Body language is central to developing trust, a lesson Boškailo learned from both Mary Fabri and his colleague in Phoenix, the psychologist Dawn Noggle. Even when she does not speak the language, Dawn reaches patients. She learns a few words of their language and makes light conversation before the interpreter arrives. Boškailo witnessed her talking to a woman from Afghanistan who suffered from severe trauma. Noggle gave a brief greeting in Pashtun and the woman hugged her, sat down, and started crying. People recognize when someone cares.

When Boškailo asked Emila and her son where they lived, Boškailo knew something was up from the pained look on both their faces. It turned out that a settlement worker had set them up in an apartment owned by a Serb. He was a good man, Boškailo had heard, an honest businessman. But the very presence of a Serb terrified his patient. Boškailo explained to them that they would not lose their benefits if they moved to another place. They left within three months.

The son said Emila seemed less anxious in her new home, and that in itself was progress. Still, the therapy moved more slowly than Boškailo would have liked, leaving him to wonder once again whether he could help Emila find any relief. She could not seem to respond to the simplest questions. Each week, she would say one or two words before turning to her son.

"How do you sleep?" Boškailo asked.

"Not good," she said, and her son filled in the details about her restless nights.

"Do you have nightmares?"

"Yes."

"Do you have headaches?"

"Yes."

The list of questions continued. Because Boškailo thought Emila looked too thin, he asked if she was eating three meals a day. Did they both take vitamins? Did they get their blood pressure checked and cholesterol levels monitored? Did Emila get mammograms? He always asked patients whether they used drugs or drank alcohol, even those who would not be obvious candidates for addiction. He talked to them about the importance of exercise and sleeping on a regular schedule, limiting caffeine and avoiding naps.

He spent a few minutes each session talking to them about PTSD and depression, and educating them on basic health issues. Such patient education was a staple of all kinds of treatment for PTSD. Sometimes home visits were in order to educate the family. He had gone several times to the house of a woman prone to flashbacks so he could demonstrate to the family how they could prevent a flashback or bring her back to the present with the scent of aromatic coffee and soothing language.

The son was listening and nodding. Emila was sitting now, much to Boškailo's relief, but she was still staring into the abyss. Sometimes he felt he was helping the son more than the mother.

Boškailo tried broaching questions about her feelings. But she would not discuss them, let alone what she had endured.

He insisted during every session on talking to her about her own trauma. He quoted Viktor Frankl and told her that she was having a normal reaction to an abnormal situation.

"You are not crazy," he said to her again and again. She had no reason to feel shame, that hard-to-comprehend, painful feeling about the self that arises in victims who bear no responsibility for tragic events. She had done nothing to cause the violence. She was not responsible for the loss.

He also told her that if she wanted to talk about what had happened, he was ready to listen. He knew it would take enormous courage to tell a story like hers to a person she did not know. There was the fear of not being believed, of breaking down, of being perceived as unstable.

He had the feeling that Emila was afraid she would be pushed into talking about Srebrenica. He had always worried that Fabri would force him to talk about the camps. So he repeatedly assured Emila that there was no rush and that it was her choice to decide when to talk. He believed that ever so slowly they were developing the kind of caring and stable relationship that would help her regain trust.

He did not have a typically Western concept of time, and neither did she.

Boškailo found it encouraging that Emila kept coming back. She seemed to find some comfort in sitting with Boškailo and her son, and answering short questions that showed concern. She even began making occasional eye contact, though never for any length of time.

"What do you do during the day?" Boškailo asked.

"Watch TV."

"What time does your son come home from work?

"Six."

"So you wait for him all day."

"Yes."

She was afraid to go to ESL classes, let alone work.

He did not remember exactly when Emila began talking in sentences. It was then that he noticed the melodic inflection in her voice and her sweet half smile, which helped him see why her son was so devoted. Once he caught her touching her son's arm gently, and he seemed pleased. Most of the time she was no longer clutching her chest so tightly, as if she could not let down her guard for a moment. Like many of his patients, she seemed to be getting younger. Her face looked less gray. Her clothes were certainly less gray and her skirts were shorter. She wasn't dressing in bright colors, but she was no longer looking like a grandmother.

It was a year before Emila broached the subject of Srebrenica, out of the blue, as if it were the most natural thing in the world.

"I'm from Srebrenica. You know that I lost my father, my husband, brother, and uncle," she said, as if she had told him many times before.

"Yes," he said. He waited several moments for her to continue.

But she did not go on. She just looked at him, more intently than she ever had before.

"You already know what happened," she said finally.

And he did. Everyone in Bosnia knew. Dozens of patients had told him similar stories of watching the hand grenades, seeing bodies flying, or running through the mountains without food or water.

"I have heard from other people it was terrible, and I am very sorry," he said, though it did not seem nearly enough.

Again he waited for her to continue. But she sat back in her chair and folded her hands in her lap.

It took several minutes for Boškailo to realize that she had no intention of continuing. Perhaps she was content to share the rest of the memory with him in silence.

"I am from Srebrenica." That was the story, her whole story, and her sense of relief was palpable.

————

One of the most important ingredients in healing is the passage of time, Boškailo believed. He had no doubt that Emila needed a doctor to help her process her trauma. But she needed time to discover the inner resources that had helped her to survive a massacre—what Richard Mollica describes as the "core will to survive and recover."

"This not-so-mysterious force which lies within . . . all of us," he writes, "is the biological, psychological and social power of self-healing, that innate capacity possessed by all human beings to re-store their physical and mental self to a state of full productivity and quality of life, no matter how severe the initial damage."

Boškailo saw the force in Emila that had been hidden for too long.

He knew she was feeling more secure when she began speaking for herself rather than letting her son answer questions. Another indication of progress was her willingness to accept the young Bosnian woman her son wanted to marry. She was a warm, beautiful young woman, who could have been threatening to a mother dependent on her only living male relative. Instead, Emila embraced her like a daughter.

This alliance with a stranger was greatly encouraging to Boškailo, a sign that Emila could form a healthy relationship outside the immediate family.

Soon, Emila was letting her future daughter-in-law accompany her to therapy sessions. Emila was clearly proud that this young woman thought enough of her future mother-in-law to take her to the doctor.

Frankl often spoke directly with his patients on the subject of finding meaning. But his was not the language that Emila would have recognized. She did not need to know that experts talked about how people find meaning in relationships. She had already embraced a new relationship that gave her hope.

When Boškailo and Emila talked about what had brought her happiness before the massacre, it did not surprise him that the answer was her family. They talked about family gatherings and how she loved making Bosnian food. She never mentioned her husband. But she did talk briefly about her first son, who had died. Boškailo did not ask questions, and she did not offer more information.

She said it once. That was enough.

Eventually her son married and he and his wife had a child. Emila was very happy about her new role as grandmother. She told her son she wanted grandchildren, many of them, as soon as possible. She had lost the role of wife, daughter, sister, and niece. Now she felt useful again.

In time Emila began coming to therapy sessions by herself. She was never a big talker, but she liked to tell stories about her grandchild. She and Boškailo began meeting once a month, and then every three months.

When he had first seen her, Boškailo would not have imagined that Emila would ever have the strength to return to Bosnia. But she told him she had one piece of unfinished business before she could go on with her new life. When the forensics team in Bosnia notified her that they had found the remains of her husband, she and her son returned home to bury him.

Had she suddenly developed a different view of life? No, she had developed what Frankl calls a tragic optimism, which allowed her to have hope in the midst of sadness. Judith Herman said it best when describing her patient: "Her view of life may be tragic, but for that very reason she has learned to cherish laughter. She has a clear sense of what is important and what is not. Having encountered evil, she knows how to cling to what is good. Having encountered the fear of death, she knows how to celebrate life."

———

Boškailo's work only heightened his sense of having survived against the odds. Just a few years earlier, he had stood in his underwear with hundreds of emaciated bodies in a concentration camp. He had lost his home, his profession, and, he worried, his family. He thought he could die at any moment. Now he was a psychiatrist helping people who had survived similar or worse torments than his own. He had patients who had spent years going to doctors who failed to recognize their traumas. He could help them because he had seen what they had seen. He had heard what they had heard.

His patients reminded him that he, too, could not escape the process of acknowledging his losses. During his time in the concentration camp, literally everything he had had before had been taken away from him, from the freedom to play with his children to his ability to practice medicine. In the camp, he could not even go to the bathroom alone.

Later he was forced to leave his country, which he considered one of the worst traumas a person could survive. It was not about nationalism. It was about leaving one's home, one's friends, one's holidays, one's culture.

Perhaps the toughest thing to lose was a belief in people. He did not know how people could inflict such pain on one another. He would never know. But he hung on to the knowledge that under the worst circumstances he himself could not inflict suffering on another person, not even if someone threatened to take his life. He believed strongly that people could be taught not to fight violence with violence, and he reminded his patients, like Emir, of the people who kept their humanity in the face of atrocities.

During his first years out of the camp he thought very little about that humanity. He had been in a concentration camp, and that was his identity.

Then he met Mary Fabri. She had never been tortured in a concentration camp. She had never been held against her will. But she listened. When he found one good person, he could begin to believe in humanity again. Sometimes it just takes one person, and that person can be a therapist.

CHAPTER 15

Here I Am without Myself

Now here I am
Without myself
Bitter
How can I go back
To whence I sprang?
  —Mak Dizdar

Adnan sat back in the leather chair as if challenging Boškailo
to pick a fight. He was a man in his fifties with a medium build,
short blond hair, and bright blue eyes. He might have looked like a
movie star had he ever bothered to shave and shower.

He was a card player and a gambler, Boškailo learned, and
Adnan sized up the doctor as if he were figuring his odds. He had
a "don't mess with me" attitude that would make him difficult to
like in the best of circumstances.

He did not want to be there, and he told Boškailo he did not
want to be there. His wife and two children were making him
come because they thought his anger was out of control. He was
so irritable, his wife told him, that they could no longer tolerate
having him in the house. He raised his voice at the slightest provocation. In fact, he did not even need provocation.

"Then why did you agree to come?" Boškailo asked him. "Nobody forced you to walk in the door."

"Leave me alone," he said, and Boškailo suspected he was used
to barking orders.

"I would leave you alone, but your family worries about you."

It was hard for Boškailo to get much of an idea who Adnan was
given his level of hostility, but he did not begrudge him that anger.

Citizens of countries hosting refugees from war-torn countries often expect them to be grateful. But people who survive trauma are often very irritable and angry, and those emotions need to be acknowledged as a normal part of the healing process.

Boškailo already knew that Adnan had spent time in Dretelj. From Boškailo's hangar, he could see the men in four other hangars. Usually Boškailo had trouble recognizing faces, but Adnan was striking with his fair good looks. He suspected that Adnan might know he had also been in Dretelj, which presented a challenge in the therapy.

In Bosnia Adnan had worked in a clothing factory. Now, like so many other survivors, he was unemployed and spending his days in the house. His wife was going to school and working as a hotel housekeeper to support the family. In Adnan's mind, this was not the way it was supposed to be.

Such arrangements were all too common in refugee families. Somebody played the role of the sick person, and the rest of the family members compensated. Boškailo knew many couples back in Bosnia who divorced after the war. In the United States, families seemed to stick together to survive after trauma.

"If anybody in the world has a right to be angry, it's you," he told Adnan.

His first sessions with Adnan were short. He reminded Boškailo that he did not want to be there.

"You can leave anytime during the session," Boškailo told him. So Adnan stayed ten minutes and left.

"How can I help you?" Boškailo asked at the beginning of the next session.

"Can I go?" Adnan would answer. But the routine was getting old even for Adnan. So each session he stayed a little longer, as if he were in training.

Within a month Adnan acknowledged that he was coming of his own volition.

Boškailo suggested that Adnan take medicine for depression. But Boškailo was not surprised when he resisted. It was hard enough for Adnan to see a doctor each week, let alone take pills that proved he was crazy. But finally he relented, and within a few weeks of taking the medicine, he had to admit he was feeling a little better.

"I'm a little less tense," he said.

Boškailo considered whether to bring up his own experience in Dretelj with Adnan, but the issue of self-disclosure was a tricky one. Some doctors consider personal disclosure a trespassing of boundaries. But the psychiatrist Andrei Novac has called on therapists to reveal their own experiences with trauma, as a way of presenting their "credentials" to patients.

Still, Novac is in favor of setting limits. Doctors and patients should not suddenly become friends who socialize outside the office. But he calls for empathy and flexibility, and he feels that doctors should choose how much to reveal to each patient.

Boškailo did not want Adnan to be burdened by the weight of his experience. He did not want Adnan to feel responsible for taking care of him. But he decided that if Adnan found out from someone in the Bosnian community that Boškailo had been in Dretelj and had not told him, Adnan would likely feel betrayed.

So Boškailo broached the subject gently.

"You were in Dretelj," Boškailo said. "So was I."

Adnan did not seem surprised or even comforted by the presence of a fellow survivor. Boškailo knew that it would be pointless at that time to ask Adnan to talk in any depth about his experience at Dretelj, the months that had stripped him of everything that mattered.

"You already know what happened," Adnan said.

Boškailo could not help thinking of Emila, who did not feel the need to voice what was already known.

And that might have been enough. Adnan might have felt relieved to be understood by his doctor. Perhaps in time he would offer more details. Perhaps some of the anger would dissipate. But Boškailo sensed that it was not just the trauma of confinement that fueled Adnan's anger. So he asked him to talk about his life before the war.

"How did you spend your days in Bosnia?"

Adnan said that each day he worked about six hours at a clothing factory. Afterward he met the same friends at a café bar, where they drank coffee and played cards. The person who lost bought a round of coffee. Later Adnan enjoyed dinner with his wife and children.

For forty years he had started his morning by reading a newspaper. He loved reading the newspaper.

"It was an excellent life," Boškailo said.

This simple acknowledgment seemed to touch Adnan. And it was the memories of the good life that began to help him feel better. He had been forced to assume the identity of a concentration camp victim. But memories validated that he had once had a different role and that he had found enjoyment in simple pleasures.

Frankl talked about one of the most noble ways of finding meaning, "by experiencing another human being in his very uniqueness, by loving him." So Boškailo asked Adnan to think about the people he still enjoyed. He loved his wife, he said, and wanted to take her out more. It meant a lot to him that his children had gone to school and found good jobs. He wanted to be closer to them, to spend more time talking with them, maybe have dinner in a restaurant.

Perhaps he could spend more time with men in the Bosnian community, he told Boškailo. He would love to play cards again, even if it was not quite the same.

He had no great book to write, and he was not planning to go to The Hague to testify.

Boškailo knew that Adnan had made progress when he started sleeping through the night. He began going on walks, sometimes with his wife, sometimes alone. He was also less irritable during the day, and he reported that he rarely lashed out at his family.

Adnan still spoke in short, crisp sentences that revealed little emotion, and Boškailo could not remember ever hearing him laugh. But Boškailo always noticed the physical changes in his patients. Adnan was more relaxed than he had been. He had let his guard down. Every statement was no longer an order.

When Adnan started shaving again, Boškailo knew there was reason to celebrate. He looked like a movie star, albeit an aging one, with sparkling blue eyes.

After six months Adnan decided to return to Bosnia for a visit.

When he returned he told Boškailo how much he had enjoyed sipping coffee in the old café bar. Boškailo could taste the thick Turkish coffee and hear sevdah playing in the background. And Adnan was ready to go on his way.

––––––––––

Sometimes Boškailo's patients found meaning after terror only to lose it, so the task of discovering a purpose had to begin again. Anna was a patient in her forties from Sarajevo. Her husband had been killed, and she had survived with her seven- and ten-year-old sons. Her whole purpose had been to save her children, and she had risked her life on a daily basis when she left home to find food and water. As the end of the war approached she was able to leave Bosnia with her sons and come to the United States. She found a good job and was doing well emotionally until about ten years later.

When her sons reached their twenties, they no longer appreciated how she had fought for them. She was in her forties and losing her children. She became severely depressed and developed PTSD symptoms. She cried all day and threatened to kill herself as memories of the war filled her days.

She arrived at the clinic, and Boškailo agreed to treat her if she signed a contract promising not to take her life.

"Many survivors are suicidal at some point," he told me, "and we teach them that they can choose whether to keep on living for their own sake or the sake of friends and family members. Some patients hold tightly to their prerogative to end their lives as it represents their last vestige of control. We ask them to choose life with the same kind of fervor."

––––––––––

How does Boškailo know when a patient is getting better? In the medical model the idea is to quantify, and Boškailo relies heavily on research that measures the efficacy of PTSD treatments (for example, cognitive therapy and eye movement desensitization and reprocessing, or EMDR) in the United States and abroad.

But he doesn't like the word "recover." He says, "It suggests that we have brought people back to their pretraumatized state. You had something and you got over it. I do not like the word 'acceptance' either, as if we have stopped protesting the unthinkable. I prefer the word 'integration,' because it does not suggest we will ever be free of trauma's grip or that a broken soul will ever really be unbroken. We have integrated the trauma experience into our lives."

He urges survivors to remember that no one can take away the experience that is uniquely theirs. He says, "Frankl talked about weaving the slender threads of a broken life into a firm pattern of meaning and responsibility."

Survivors, Robert Jay Lifton noted, may find meaning in the realization that their experience, however horrible, has been "illuminating in its pain." There is a sense of "victory over the forces of destruction" and a realization that one's pain has been shared by others and can be integrated into a larger understanding and political context.

In addition, Judith Herman wrote that "recovery is based not on the illusion that evil has been overcome, but rather on the knowledge that it has not entirely prevailed and that restorative love may still be found in the world."

Helping patients grapple with their questions of meaning has helped Boškailo become more accepting of his own role as both survivor and healer.

"I am finally able to say out loud that I am a concentration camp survivor. It is part of my story. The experience is a part of me, and it made me stronger. If you took away the concentration camp, I would no longer be Esad."

CHAPTER 16
Take No Pity

Take no pity; let's go
kill that scum down in the city
—Radovan Karadžić

Boškailo, Aiša, and I had planned to spend three days in The Hague attending the trial of Dr. Radovan Karadžić, the Bosnian Serb leader charged with genocide committed in Srebrenica in July 1995 and with crimes against humanity. We also wanted to interview the staff of the victim protection unit of the International Criminal Tribunal of the Former Yugoslavia (ICTY). We had already attended a national war crimes trial involving lower-rank leaders in Sarajevo, but Boškailo had walked out in less than ten minutes.

Tensions were high when we reached the city. We were tired of each other, and we were anxious about facing one of the world's leading war criminals.

"I would not be here," Boškailo said, "if it wasn't for the book." There would be nothing healing about facing Karadžić, he told me. He would rather be anywhere else in the world.

Early on in the project, Boškailo had told me, "I feel good about doing this." Now he was tired of my relentless questioning and immersion into an era he would rather not relive.

I found myself forgetting that Boškailo was vulnerable to the same stresses he had felt at the beginning of our interviews, as if our work together had somehow "cured" him. He had told me that for many people PTSD is a lifelong vulnerability. But at six-foot-two he looked so invulnerable, especially when he was with Aiša, her arm in his, a reminder that he had found his way home.

I dressed up for our trip to the court. Boškailo wore jeans, as if to say Karadžić did not deserve our respect.

We took a seat behind a clear partition and watched Karadžić take his seat. Now two psychiatrists sat in the courtroom, separated only by bulletproof glass: Dr. Esad Boškailo, a concentration camp survivor turned healer, and Dr. Radovan Karadžić, a Serbian war criminal.

Despite his protests, I knew Boškailo wanted to witness history, and we both wanted to learn whether justice for survivors could be found in a courtroom. But he resented the fact that it had taken thirteen years to find Karadžić, who was not arrested until July 2008. The former president of the Serbian Republic, the head of the Serbian Democratic Party, and the supreme commander of the Bosnian Serb army, Karadžić had been hiding out in a small Serbian town as a New Age natural healer. Known as Dragan Dabić, he wore a full beard, long gray hair gathered in a top knot, and a long overcoat.

Slobodan Milošević had died on March 11, 2006, in the detention center while on trial in The Hague. At the time, Boškailo had been more resigned than euphoric.

"I was in the gym playing basketball in Phoenix, and I got a text message from my wife that he died. I saved the message for a long time. Then I just felt numb and kept on playing basketball. I'm not happy that he died, but it's the natural ending for war criminals. He died in his cell, that's the most important fact about him. He died in prison. That should be a message to everybody who tries to kill others. He thought he could kill and live forever. I talked to a few Bosnian friends to ask them how they felt. Nobody was excited. Nobody had any big thoughts. He died in his cell, and I was playing basketball."

Through the glass in the courtroom, we saw a clean-shaven, heftier Karadžić wearing a dark blue suit. His chin was covered with red marks, as if he had been picking at scabs. But he had not neglected his gray and white locks, shorter now and combed into the pompadour he was famous for during the war. He was representing himself during the trial, with the assistance of Serbian and American lawyers.

Boškailo sat at the edge of his chair in the observation area, less a sign of concentration, I thought, than a guarantee he could flee. Fifteen people sat in the courtroom while ten of us watched from the witness section. Three judges in black and red robes sat at the head of the circular room. To their right was Karadžić in the second row, an armed guard at his side. The witness stood at a podium in the center with his back to us.

Boškailo stared through the glass at the aging commander and was convinced that Karadžić met his gaze. "He probably thinks I'm Serbian because I'm tall and have a beard," Boškailo said.

Karadžić was determined to prove the remarks he made in his opening statement on March 1, 2010. "They're trying to convict us for something we never did," he said. "There is no Serb responsibility. . . . I will defend that nation of ours and their cause, which is just and holy." The Serbs, he claimed, were the ones that had made concessions to preserve the peace. Muslims, he said, were responsible for war, and the genocide had never occurred.

Milan Mandilović, the medical director of the state hospital in Sarajevo during the war, was the first witness that day, July 19, 2010. The doctor testified that the Serbs had cut off water and medical supplies to Bosniaks in the city, and Karadžić wanted to show they had done no such thing.

"Do you, Doctor, reject the possibility that Muslim authorities sabotaged the possibility of repairing the water supply and making water available?" Karadžić asked Mandilović.

Mandilović replied, "I don't believe the forces of the federal part of Sarajevo were involved in any acts of sabotage. It wasn't in the interest of the population that lived there."

For several minutes Karadžić fumbled through a stack of papers and asked Mandilović to point out landmarks on a series of maps projected on the courtroom screen. He was trying to prove that the Serbian army positioned at the Jewish cemetery could not see the Sarajevo state hospital. But anyone from Sarajevo knew that the Serbs could have seen the hospital, given that it was the tallest building in the area.

When a judge objected to the tedious process of having a witness point out recognized locations, Karadžić justified his Columbo-like defense. "Have a bit of faith in my lawyerly skills," said Karadžić, who had no legal training. "I know exactly what I'm trying to say and what I'm trying to show, and we cannot settle that out of court."

"Unbelievable," Esad said a little too loudly. "It's masturbation in the justice system."

The pace of the proceedings was mind-numbingly slow, and court officers estimated that at this rate the trial could last for years. But Boškailo knew if he was going to be a witness to history, he had to sit through a few hours of testimony.

In the following days, Hussein Ali Abdel-Razek, who served as a commander of the UN Protection Force in Sarajevo, appeared as a witness. He read from an August 1992 report by Tadeusz Mazowiecki, a UN emissary, describing the conditions of the times.

"[Sarajevo] is shelled on a regular basis in what appears to be a deliberate attempt to spread terror among the population. Snipers shoot innocent civilians. The mission visited the hospital and was able to see many civilian victims. It was able to see the damage done to the hospital itself, which has been deliberately shelled on several occasions, despite the proper display of the internationally recognized Red Cross symbol. . . .

"There was terror on their faces; people were terrorized, and I felt people running in terror out of fear of snipers. And we, at the United Nations, we were also subject to sniping as we moved in the streets. Life was very bad and very desperate, especially for civilians in the Sarajevo region."

Karadžić seemed unmoved by the vivid description of warfare. The Serbs, he told the judges, were not to blame for the violence.

Boškailo left the courtroom as Karadžić was sorting through more papers. "That was three hours of wasting our time," Boškailo said. "He doesn't talk about when he was in uniform shooting at us. He doesn't talk about victims. Crazy Karadžić, he never made any sense."

At the end of the day, Boškailo met Mario Barfus, a lanky, blond man in his forties who worked in the office of the president of the ICTY. In the 1990s he had been a field worker in the International Committee of the Red Cross, responsible for "war-affected territories of the former Yugoslavia." He registered prisoners at the camps throughout Bosnia, monitored the conditions in which they lived, asked them about the quality and quantity of the food, provided basic medication (and, when possible, mailed letters from prisoners), and monitored prisoner exchanges.

Mario had stood in the front door of Gabela each night for a stretch. The guards would not let him in, but he was a reminder that some people in the world were watching.

"At least now I don't have to ask you how you liked the food," Barfus said to Boškailo as he put his arm around the former prisoner.

That evening, over a leisurely dinner, Boškailo and Barfus reminisced about the war, debating whether one could make generalizations about the Croats in southern Bosnia. They did not say anything about the camps. They didn't have to.

"When you visited, why didn't you take me with you?" Boškailo asked his new friend, one of the few people who understood the life he had led.

Later, Barfus said the visits to the prisons had been agonizing in a region once respected for its diversity. "The prisoners were a symbol of my own identity vanishing. And the possibility of keeping prisoners alive was a duty to the state in which I was born. This feeling combined with extreme anger kept me going."

———

"Justice is ideal, and The Hague is far from ideal," Boškailo told me the next morning. "I admire the people working in the criminal tribunal in The Hague and the international community for trying to do something, but it really does not make sense to talk about justice.

"Karadžić is the only one here. What about the other ten thousand people who are not here? Some people think if they send Karadžić to jail for thirty years it's perfect. Well, it's far from perfect. What do I get from that? Having him on death row would not bring a tenth of one percent of justice. It doesn't give me back my friends and relatives who were killed. It doesn't give back the arms and legs of two thousand children wounded in Sarajevo. My cousin who lost her child doesn't care if Karadžić gets five years or twenty-five.

"People think I should be happy because Karadžić is on trial. Well, I'm not happy. I wish I'd never known this guy. I wish he'd never existed. The international community should have done a better job of preventing this war."

"What about Nuremberg?" I asked. "You had said that thinking about Nuremberg gave you hope in the camps."

"Nuremberg was different," he said. "The German people had to accept that they lost the war. Hitler was killed. The United States, France, and England stayed together. Here we have people who were responsible for concentration camps still in power. We have cities like Stolac and Čapljina where there are separate schools for Bosniaks and Croats."

"Would you testify if you're called?"

"Yes," he said, without hesitation. "I'm not a hero, but I would defend my time on the front line. But testifying is high risk, even for your children. I come from a small town where everybody knows me. Even if they disguised me, everyone in the community would know I had talked."

If a trial was insufficient, he said, it was still a necessity to let future killers know they would face the consequences of their actions. "Will there be reconciliation and forgiveness? I don't think so. The average Bosnian does not have much trust in the tribunal. But the court may bring closure. People can start living together again. We can just hope the new generation does not want war."

His only comfort, he said, was that Karadžić was returning to a locked cell with defendants, some of whom were former enemies, while he and Aiša went to their comfortable hotel. Two psychiatrists were going their separate ways.

"I am free and he is not."

The act of testifying at a war crimes trial is therapeutic for witnesses, many observers presume. Seeing the accused sitting under armed guard, telling one's story in a safe space, and hearing a judge pronounce a guilty verdict, it is assumed, will give survivors a sense of closure, if not justice.

But few people have actually asked witnesses whether the experience of testifying has been cathartic or traumatic. It's a question therapists like Boškailo grapple with when they prepare survivors who want to go The Hague.

For his patients, the experience has been largely positive, but his sampling of patients is too small to draw any definitive conclusions about whether participating in a war-crimes tribunal helps survivors heal after terror.

Eric Stover, the scholar and longtime human-rights activist, conducted the most comprehensive and revealing study when he interviewed eighty-seven witnesses in The Hague. Of those interviewed, 77 percent said it had been a positive experience. But Stover noted that little attention had been paid to witnesses once they returned to their communities in the former Yugoslavia, and some of them had suffered reprisals. The few witnesses he interviewed who described testifying as cathartic found that "the glow quickly faded when they returned to their villages and towns." And the short sentences handed down to perpetrators left many feeling that justice had not prevailed.

Courtrooms, he noted, are "hardly safe and secure environments for the recounting of traumatic events." And rarely are survivors allowed to tell their entire stories. But during the past two decades tribunals and truth commissions have tried to cushion the experience for survivors, with varying degrees of success.

We met with the managers of the support unit of the victim and witness protection section of the ICTY, which has forty employees, most of whom are based in The Hague. Helena Vranov Schoorl was trained as a social worker and now works as a support officer for the section, which impressed Boškailo because of its focus on meeting the client's psychological and social needs.

The team does not provide therapy; there isn't time for that. But a member of the team is available around the clock to assist people testifying.

"We don't want them to feel abandoned in The Hague," Schoorl told us. So they comfort those who felt the defense counsels prevented them from telling their whole story. They deal with flashbacks and anxiety attacks. They take witnesses for long walks on the beach.

Victims of sexual crimes may be allowed to testify at the ICTY by one-way, closed-circuit television, so they do not have to see their alleged perpetrators. In a few cases, victim and witness protection relocates people who might face retaliation were they to return home.

Many witnesses reported immediate relief when they testified at the ICTY, but there was no telling how they would feel back in their communities six months down the line.

"Did testifying help or hurt people psychologically?" I asked Schoorl.

"We argue about that every day," she said.

———

During a speech at Oxford University, Karadžić's lawyer-adviser Peter Robinson, who describes himself as a "fighter for human rights," called his client a man with charisma "in spades." He was a poet, Robinson noted, and a psychiatrist. "He's very religious in the Serbian Orthodox Church. . . . He's very funny. He's very, very bright."

When Robinson told me that Karadžić had been given permission by the court to answer—or refuse to answer—questions posed to him via e-mail that were approved by the court, Boškailo and I agreed that I would write to him asking a question that would also appeal to his vanity: "Drawing upon your experience as a psychiatrist and natural healer, how have you found meaning after war?"

A few weeks later we got our court-approved answer in the form of a rambling four-page missive that loosely addressed the issue of meaning. Once again Karadžić presented the Serbs as victims who were fighting fundamentalist Muslim aggressors. The Serbs' reason for being, he maintained, was defending "Freedom."

"In the Bosnian civil war the Serbs' 'beautiful Helen' [of Troy] was Freedom," Karadžić wrote. "And none of the 1.5 million of the Serbs in [Bosnia] didn't wonder about the price. And the price was the most precious one: the lives of the best part of this small community. Why did they accept the probability of loosing [sic] their dearest? What was the sense of the war for them? Every one of them would tell you without delay that it was the highest value of their own lives—Freedom. . . . They fought for freedom without denying any rights to the others."

He continued: "Who cares that we suffered four years for nothing, since the Muslims have no regard for the rest of the world."

In the most surprising section of the letter, Karadžić praised the people he considered to be "highly moral and independent spirits." Among them were the late English playwright Harold Pinter, the late Russian writer Aleksandr Solzhenitsyn, the scholar and activist Noam Chomsky, and the journalist Diana Johnstone.

Pinter and Solzhenitsyn had opposed Western intervention in Serbia. Pinter had signed an open letter calling for the release of Slobodan Milošević from the war crimes tribunal in The Hague.

Chomsky had signed a public letter opposing the decision of a Swedish publisher to withdraw Diana Johnstone's *Fools' Crusade: Yugoslavia, NATO and Western Delusions*, a book the signers called "an outstanding work."

In her book, Johnstone wrote that "the hypothesis can at least be advanced that whatever crimes were committed by Serb forces were in violation of Karadžić's orders and without his consent." She said that what the court called a genocide was "perhaps only a brutal little civil war for control of contiguous territory." The descriptions of camps and the number of reported war victims had been greatly exaggerated, she wrote, and Western journalists had been duped.

Critics, such as the *Guardian* correspondent Ed Vulliamy, who was among those who first saw the camps, accused Chomsky of failing to acknowledge the scope of the horror and of providing comfort to Karadžić.

Chomsky later said that he had never denied the Srebrenica massacre. And when I sent him an e-mail asking him to comment on Karadžić's message to us, Chomsky said he had no idea what the doctor had in mind.

Karadžić, Chomsky wrote, is "surely a war criminal."

I was not surprised that Boškailo had no desire to participate in the debate. He had no comment on whether Bosnians had suffered enough.

Boškailo thought of Karadžić as a doctor without giving much thought to his career as a psychiatrist. I was more fascinated by the history of a war criminal who once tried to soothe troubled souls.

Karadžić, who fancied himself an artist despite critical condemnation, is known for such poems as "A Morning Hand Grenade."

Surprisingly little has been written about Karadžić the psychiatrist. The American Psychiatric Association passed a motion condemning him for "brutal and inhumane actions." During the 1970s, he sold fraudulent medical diagnoses. In 1985 he was arrested for fraud and embezzlement of public property. He was imprisoned only briefly.

Ismet Cerić, clinic director at Kosovo Hospital, where Karadžić began working as a psychiatrist, told the producers of the PBS *Frontline* documentary "The World's Most Wanted Man" that Karadžić never distinguished himself as a doctor.

"I must say that he as a psychiatrist was ordinary. . . . [He] is not hard worker. He tried to find the easy way for everything."

Another Serbian psychiatrist, Jovan Rašković, was the first president of the Serbian Democratic Party, and he was known for his nationalistic speeches. Rašković was widely quoted as saying, "Serbs are crazy people."

"And when a psychiatrist tells you you're crazy," Boškailo said, "you are really crazy."

I also reread Robert Jay Lifton's groundbreaking book *The Nazi Doctors* in search of patterns among doctors who practiced "killing in the name of healing." Lifton introduced the concept of "doubling," when doctors participated in atrocities by day while playing congenial husbands and fathers at home. Doubling, Lifton wrote, permitted them to commit atrocities without viewing themselves as evil or having feelings of guilt. He singled out the Nazi Max de Crinis, who "inwardly maintained his sense of being a proper academic psychiatrist" while practicing "euthanasia."

I also found it interesting that the Nazis had a particular interest in natural healers, who, Lifton wrote, "appealed to the regime's biological romanticism and mysticism." I imagined the bearded Karadžić waving his hands around his patients to balance their energy flows. And then I pictured a man with an Elvis coif languishing in a jail cell.

CHAPTER 17
The Dead Who Are Living

He died many long years ago
He died but he's still
Not dead
    —Mak Dizdar

I think of the dead
who are living
    —Fahrudin Zilkić, Bosnian poet (1968–)

Women in mourning, some stooped from age and grief, stood over newly dug graves in a field of graves as wide as we could see. In front of us, a painfully thin woman in a long white veil wailed as if she had lost her loved one the night before. Young children who had never seen war held onto her arms, as if she might jump into the pit.

Boškailo and Aiša had no bodies to bury at Srebrenica in the summer of 2008. They were not like Boškailo's patient Emila, who had waited year after year to learn from the forensic experts that they had found her husband in a mass grave and she could bury him. But Boškailo, Aiša, and I wanted to honor the victims of the worst massacre since World War II, when some eight thousand Muslim men and boys were killed over several days in 1995.

Three thousand victims are buried at the center, which consists of a large cemetery of graves marked with uniform white headstones and a row of marble blocks on which the name of the victims are engraved.

By the time we arrived in the late morning on a scorching July day, tens of thousands of people had gathered to bury 308 more genocide victims. The youngest victim buried that day was fifteen, and the oldest eighty-four. Hundreds of mourners had arrived after a four-day peace march. They had followed the route taken by fifteen thousand men trying to escape the slaughter by fleeing toward Tuzla. Many were killed by Serb army and police personnel.

Now their children and grandchildren carried Bosnian flags in their names. They would come back year after year until all the dead were buried, and they would raise their own children to return every July 11.

Boškailo went down the hill to pray with thousands of men. We could see them kneeling on their assorted prayer mats, raising and lowering their bodies in unison. Aiša, wearing a headscarf—the first time I had seen her in one—and I sat on the grass in the hot sun next to women with parasols.

Our eyes were fixed on the sea of green, row upon row of green caskets, each identified with a number, as if to prevent the bodies from getting lost again. Women touched the caskets gently or draped themselves on them. They wanted the souls of their loved ones to rest in peace. But it was wrenching to say goodbye again.

We watched as groups of three or more men gathered around each casket and lifted it on their shoulders. Slowly, they carried the caskets to the edge of the field and walked in procession around the memorial site as mourners reached out to touch the coffins.

Srebrenica was supposed to have been a safe place, not a gravesite.

In March 1993 the commander of the UN peacekeeping troops had personally led a convoy of trucks to the surrounded area and promised that the United Nations would protect it.

But in July 1995 Serb troops led by General Ratko Mladić overran the area. The Dutch UN troops were outnumbered and failed to protect the town. They watched as Mladić's troops rounded up the population of Srebrenica, then deported the women and children to government-controlled territory and took the men away for execution.

The International Court of Justice in The Hague ruled that the actions at Srebrenica were genocide. Secretary General Kofi

Annan called it one of the darkest days in the United Nations' history. Yet many Serbs (and others) still deny the magnitude of the killings.

At the burial, dignitaries gave speeches we strained to hear on the distant loudspeakers.

"We expect Serbia . . . to arrest as soon as possible and hand over all those who took part in this genocide project," said Bosnian president Haris Silajdžić.

The U.S. ambassador to Bosnia and Herzegovina, Charles English, also spoke. He was the first U.S. ambassador to be invited to the service.

"I am humbled by the heavy task of addressing so heinous a crime and so profound a grief," he said. "Nowhere else, and at no time before have I felt so intensely the futility of words. Words fail here. But there is one word, and only one word, that can describe what happened in and around Srebrenica in July 1995. That word is genocide."

Mustafa Cerić, head of the Bosnian Islamic Community, called on the European Parliament to declare July 11 a day of mourning.

Muslims and Jews, he said, should not be persecuted on the basis of religion, nationality, or skin color. "We should pray that the tragedy of Srebrenica never happens again."

We were all moved by the mention of Jews and Muslims. But our attention quickly turned to the women, wailing for loved ones lost and found as they waited for their bodies to be returned to the earth.

I could not bring myself to interview any of the mourners, with the exception of a few young people who had participated in the peace march in memory of relatives they had never known. But the *Srebrenica Genocide Blog* features quotes from mourners at the annual memorial, including a woman named Sabaheta Fejzić, who lost her son, her husband, and father. Fejzić visited the gravesite in 2008 and said, "Every time I hear of a new grave I hope that at last my soul can rest. Many bodies were burned or thrown down the river. But for some families this place means the nightmare is over. One day it may be so for me."

A Dutch soldier, one of twelve who joined the memorial march for the first time since the massacre, told reporters that he either spent nights awake or had nightmares of the killing. He was supposed to be a peacekeeper. He never wanted to allow a tragedy to happen on his watch. And for him there was no closure.

For most of Boškailo's patients who visited the gravesite, the ritual brought a sense of finality and the beginning of healing. For Emila the belief that her husband's soul would finally find peace meant she could embrace a new life. Boškailo and Aiša felt no such comfort. For them, the memorial service was a reminder that "never again" happened again and again.

CHAPTER 18
Once Again among You

You see how good it is that I didn't die,
and that I am once again among you?
You can whistle, you can applaud.
You see how good it is that I didn't die,
and that I am once again among you all.
    —Izet Sarajlić, Bosnian poet (1930–)

I'm still here. A minute of silence for me.
    —Izet Sarajlić

We arrived in Počitelj more than fifteen years after Boškailo and his friends were released from the camps, and drove to his childhood home, a small, empty two-bedroom cement structure in need of fresh paint. He and Aiša return to the house for a couple of weeks every year or two. They sleep on mattresses on the floor and keep their clothes in their suitcases, as if to say they are only visiting.

I had wanted to contact the fellow prisoners Boškailo had lived with in the camps before we left for our trip to Bosnia. But he had convinced me that it was courting rejection to call up concentration camp survivors and ask them if they wanted to be interviewed about finding meaning after terror. We should instead invite them to talk when we ran into them in the street or the café bars.

"They're everywhere," he assured me. And so were the concentration camp guards.

Had their enemies fled the town it might have been easier to go back, he said. Instead, they were surrounded by the very people who had held them in the camps. And as if to prove his point, when we were walking down the road in Počitelj, a tanned, beefy man waved to Boškailo as if greeting an old friend.

He was the Croatian guard who had escorted Boškailo from Mostar to Dretelj.

Unnerved, Boškailo waved back. He had not expected to wave. He just did.

Closer to home was the former concentration camp guard who lived in the house behind his. He was a military policeman whom Boškailo had seen at Dretelj. Boškailo thought they had an unspoken understanding that they would never acknowledge one another's presence.

But on a hot, sunny morning, the tall, gaunt man walked up to Boškailo in his backyard.

"Come see my peppers," he said.

Boškailo followed and dutifully surveyed the rows of plants. Such was the strange aftermath of war.

The Dayton Peace Accords ending the war in 1995 had divided the country into the Federation of Bosnia and Herzegovina, made up of Bosniaks and Croatians, and the Serbian Republic, each with its own government. The result, Boškailo believed, was disastrous and could have been prevented by better planning. He had dreamed of a unique nation in Europe with three groups living together. Parceling out the state, he said, has resulted in apartheid as Croats continue to oppress Bosniaks within their own federation.

Most of the Bosniaks in his town used to work in Čapljina, a few miles away from Počitelj. Now only Croats can find work in Čapljina. Bosniaks can vote for their own political candidates, but they have to be approved by the Croats, so no Bosniak who criticizes the Croats has a chance of getting elected. Schools are divided into Bosniak and Croatian classes, and children are learning to hate one another. A new generation is blinded by nationalism.

Perhaps hatred is clearest in the sports arena. The fans of the Croatian national soccer team chant, "Fuck Bosnia. This is Croatia." And when the Serbs lose, Bosniaks sing in the streets.

We drove to the Stolac office of the Association of Concentration Camp Survivors of Bosnia-Herzegovina, where I found Osman, the president of the group, and his friend Mirsad, an electrician turned businessman. Osman and Mirsad had asked Esad to sign on to a lawsuit suing the Federation on behalf of concentration camp survivors, and he had readily agreed.

On the wall hung a black-and-white poster of prisoners in Dretelj, revealing emaciated bodies and faces with blank expressions.

"We looked like zombies when we came out of the camps," said Mirsad, who had survived Silos, Gabela, and Ljubuški. "We were so skinny and dehydrated that the officers who saw us got scared of their own creations."

He lit up a cigarette and took a long drag as if to calm himself. "I have to smoke," he said.

"When memories of the horrors return," he continued, "you find yourself stunned. I've led a fight in my head for a long time, and I've kept asking myself, 'Dear God, how is it possible a human heart can do such horrible things?' If somebody offered me the chance to do to people what was done to me, I would never be able to. When you're in this situation there's nothing you can do but find peace with yourself."

How did he find peace? I asked. In the early days he sought psychological help, he said. He took some mild tranquilizers to help him sleep. But these were just short-term fixes.

"In the end, my family is the source of joy in my life. They bring me happiness and make me go on. All I want is my three daughters to live a happy life and not go through what I went through. I live in hope that future generations in Bosnia and Herzegovina don't experience what I did."

Osman looked stout and healthy. But looks can be deceiving, he told me. His knee, broken by a guard wielding a steel rod, was still acting up. He developed diabetes while in Gabela, and heart problems as well. He had undergone four bypass operations.

He, too, takes comfort in his family, noting that the initial reunion was difficult given that his young daughter did not recognize her emaciated father. "Now all the things I love give me strength and the material doesn't count for anything. I have two grandchildren. When they run toward me and I carry them in my arms, nothing can compare to the amount of happiness I get."

He also devotes numerous hours to managing the lawsuit, which seeks for each survivor three hundred euros for every day spent in the camps. The situation is far from ideal, he notes. Legally, the survivors cannot sue the Bosnian Croats independently. They have to sue the entire Federation, which includes Bosniaks. So victims may end up paying victims for those crimes. But Osman is determined to hold the country accountable for war crimes, and determined that the survivors should receive some compensation for their pain.

"We want to make the guilty pay for what they've done. People tend to ask me when this is going to be over. I say I'll be happy if my grandson gets the money after I die. I'll be happy if he says, 'This is for my grandfather and all he and the others have done.'"

————

Boškailo and I visited the country home of Benca, the man who taught the prisoners poetry, and his wife, who served us mint juice on a porch shaded by grape leaves. The professor had entered politics, rising to serve as the president of Stolac County. Later he became head of security at a prison in Mostar.

During this period he also wrote about the camps in two books and a series of essays. "I would spend nights and nights just writing," he said. "The first book, *Stolac Is Destiny*, I wrote in two months. I just had to scream. It just came out of me. The second book took three years. I felt a big burden to tell my story. That's been lifted.

"When I finished my book I knew there was going to be trouble, but I was happy. One year after the first book I lost my job; one year after the second book I lost my job."

He could not be sure, he said, of the cause and effect. But it was clear to him that in Bosnia, criticizing Croats was risky business.

Finding that his wife, mother, and children were alive after the war brought him the greatest joy. But he feels that the war stole years of his life.

"And I lost my country," he said. "This isn't the country I wanted. This isn't the Bosnia we had. Thieves and criminals rule the state."

"Is justice possible?" I asked.

"No, justice is not possible. I can't remember the last time I've seen justice or lived justice. I can't remember anybody before me who has seen justice. I doubt anybody after me will. Justice isn't possible anywhere in the world and especially not here."

He continued, "Croats and Serbs are still acting like heroes. I haven't reached the day I saw any Serb or Croat apologize and say, 'Our guys really messed up.' The most peaceful thing they said is 'Why did we ever need this?' which means they are not truly ready for peace. I can barely wait to forgive somebody who apologizes, but nobody is saying, 'I'm sorry.' Sometimes I think they're waiting for me to say, 'I'm sorry you imprisoned me.'"

———

Alija, a journalist who edits the magazine *Hercegovacke Novine* in Mostar and runs a radio station, spoke to us in his office overlooking a stone mosque. He had been the head of information service in the Bosnia and Herzegovina Army 4th Corps, and he and Boškailo had overlapped at three of the camps.

"I never found the answer as to why people did these things to me," he said, in the booming voice he was famous for.

But Alija had been an optimist, and he remained one after all these years. He saw glimpses of justice when he provided testimony in The Hague in early 2007 against six former Bosnian Croatian leaders and about his five months in detention.

"Everything bad carries a bit of good in itself," he said. "I'm a classic example of how bad things can be used for something good. During my time in the concentration camp I got an immense psychological strength which has helped me to carry on. The evil I saw and the bad things that happened to me have helped me to understand things I never confronted before."

He continued, "I've learned four things. They are: in this life man is always alone; a man should always do things he feels in his heart are right to do; a man should have no regrets; a man should appreciate the small joys in life during the short time he is here. When I was younger I always thought to the future. In high school I dreamed of college. But there is only the moment and nothing else."

"Was testifying in The Hague such a moment?" I asked.

"Yes," he said. "I talked about the worst things that can happen to prisoners."

Of all the camps, he told the court, Dretelj was the black hole. "The nineteen days I spent there felt like nineteen thousand years." He talked about how guards used to amuse themselves by forcing prisoners to slap one another. And how they took them outside to "reeducate" them, which meant heavy beatings.

"I'd come full circle," he said of his days in The Hague. The guards who had tortured him were now at his mercy.

———

The dentist did not want to talk about the camps, but he agreed to for the sake of this book. War, he said, did not affect Bosnians as strongly as it did other people because they were used to the violence. "People in Bosnia carry war and death and bloodshed in their genes," he said, in the small waiting room outside his dental office. Still, his body tensed as he began talking in short, clipped sentences.

Like Alija he believed that the camp experience was not all negative.

"The concentration camps changed my life in a positive manner. People usually are concerned about trivial things: jobs, cars. They don't realize the true meaning of life is way beyond that. I'm still looking for it; that's part of the mystery of heaven and hell. My interest in religion existed even before the war. I was raised to be religious.

"Today I pray five times a day. I believe I am a better man than I was before the war. I used to drink alcohol. I used to hang around with a lot of people not connected to religion. I feel I have made up for the alcohol and for things I did before the war with my prayers.

"The Catholic and Orthodox have a thing called cleansing. It happens when they go to another world. They live a type of life convinced they will go through a cleansing when they die. I believe that a man should obey the commandments in this world and not the other one."

The dentist was still known throughout Herzegovina for providing free dental care for the poor. And I learned he had hired the daughter of Kapa, Boškailo's best friend, to be a dental technician. But there was no opportunity to ask more questions of the only survivor I met who talked about God. The interview was over, he said. It was time for coffee and cake.

Hivzo, the chemistry professor, was one of the few Muslims working in the predominantly Croatian county of nearby Čapljina. Only Croatian professors now staffed in the schools in which he had taught for eighteen years, so he took a job assisting returning refugees with their housing needs.

Boškailo had convinced Hivzo to talk to me at a café bar in Počitelj. He was rounder and balder than the younger man Boškailo had described. But I could still imagine the other professor, his Croatian friend, Djevenica, towering over him in the café bar.

"Do you ever see the professor who was your friend?" I asked.

"I see him a lot, but I never say hello," he said.

He paused a moment. "I will never understand it. I still cannot believe that all my neighbors and friends turned their heads and acted as if they did not know me. I cannot believe that no one came to the camp and helped me. Not just the professor. But others in Čapljina who were my friends."

Why had he not fled after the war?

"Because at that point a rebel woke up in me. I wanted to go back to the house where I was born. I wanted to show everyone I'm here. I'm back in the house I lived in before the war."

In the fields behind his house he finds the greatest pleasure. "I grow every type of fruit you can grow. I sell tomatoes, peaches, peppers."

He continued, "People find meaning in various things. I hang out with a couple of Bosnian friends in my village, and I have four children, two daughters and two sons. In the camp I found out my wife was pregnant with our fourth child. My youngest boy was born in Mostar while I was in the camp. I saw him first when he was six months old. It was the happiest moment of my life. I felt complete happiness when I saw all my children were alive in Mostar.

"Today I have six grandchildren, and they bring me great joy and satisfaction and pleasure. It's pure emotion. I find meaning in those things."

Goran, the journalist whose nickname was "Nerves," was visiting Bosnia from his adopted home in the Netherlands, where he maintains computer networks in Amsterdam. He agreed to come out for coffee, though he rarely frequented the café bars anymore. Boškailo joined us at the beginning of our talk but eventually moved to another table, as if anticipating what was to come.

When Goran and his wife had arrived in Holland fifteen years earlier, they had been determined to start a new life and never talk about the camps.

"A normal life," he said.

He went back to school and chose a profession that required more interaction with machines than with people.

"I liked my job, and I thought I had found meaning in my work."

But a decade later the memories of Bosnia he had kept at bay began returning, occasional glimpses of the past followed by a flood of memories that came on without warning. It was not long before his wife and child noticed a striking change in his behavior.

"I started reacting to things that happened around me. I became nervous and I was provoked easily. Often I would try to prove people were wrong. I started losing patience with my wife and child. I could become highly provoked when I watched television, particularly when I saw somebody lying about Bosnia.

"I saw that something was wrong with me, and I started visiting a psychiatrist. For nine months I have seen two psychiatrists once a week. I take an antidepressant, but medication doesn't help much. I don't feel any calmer.

"I keep trying to live a normal life. To keep on doing everything I've done before. When you return to Bosnia and see the faces of people who have done all this, everything restarts and you go back to the beginning.

"When I come back to Bosnia I go to the seaside with my family. And I come to the house at night to talk to my parents. I don't have contact with my Croatian neighbors. I don't go out much. I don't go to cafés much.

"I thought I found meaning in work. But I was wrong. I don't believe that meaning exists. There is too much anger, too many unanswered questions. It's all built up in me. I don't know if I will find meaning if I ever figure it out. I can't react because my entire life fell apart like a tower of cards. And whatever I do and whenever I look at anything or anyone I keep thinking about how we lived before and what it is like now. They take away your soul. They can kill you and torture you. But the worst thing that happens is taking away our soul. Without a soul you walk around like a zombie."

Goran was silent for moment. Then he looked up at me as if asking for mercy. Were we done? he wanted to know. Did I have enough information? And I saw that I had asked too much.

He got up slowly, shook my hand, and headed toward his car. Boškailo, engrossed in a conversation at another table, did not follow him. Perhaps he had not seen Goran leave or had not noticed the distraught expression on his face. Even if Boškailo had, I doubt that in the moment he could have comforted his friend. When it came to healing from trauma, Boškailo knew, months could turn into years, and years into decades. And he had no pill to take away loss.

CHAPTER 19

Evening Stroll

This evening stroll deserves a poem
   —Semezdin Mehmedinović

Is life worth living?
The answer, this Saturday, is yes
   —Ranko Sladojević, Bosnian poet (1951–)

The psychiatrist Frank Ochberg, the founder of the Dart Center for Journalism and Trauma, describes three acts in the news coverage of trauma. The first act is the news story, the straightforward reporting on a traumatic event. The second act is the human-interest story that finds some lesson from the tragedy that leaves the world inspired. The third act is the story few editors want to tell: the crisis that makes no sense, has no meaning, leaves no one any wiser.

Our story falls somewhere in the middle of acts two and three. Boškailo resents people who try to romanticize experiences of horror, as if there is any meaning to be found in holding people in concentration camps or raping women or killing children. Well-meaning platitudes about everything happening for a reason leave him wanting to shout, What kind of God would do this for a reason?

But Boškailo is a healer who believes that people can find meaning that transcends the tragedy. And he is convinced that a therapist can be the person who reminds a survivor that caring relationships are still possible.

So we are among the romantics stuck in act two who cannot escape the desire for an ending focused on hope.

"What did this project mean for you?" I asked Boškailo.

"Too many years," he said, smiling.

"It was painful, sometimes. Sometimes we laughed about being like Elaine and Jerry on *Seinfeld*, each with our own agenda. You wanted to talk. I didn't want to talk. I think we both learned how to respect each other. We listened to one another. That's what I valued most.

"For me this was about the beauty of healing, and this time my own healing. This is the first time I was able to step outside of myself and look at the camp, to talk about the camp from outside the camp. And I can continue talking about camps without feeling the same sense of dread. I don't imagine, anymore, that I will be in the middle of a conversation or alone in my office and find myself back in the camps."

He continued, "Most of all, I want people to know this should never happen again. That's why we have courts and that's why we have books. People must know that whatever the situation, they should not resort to torture. We all have choices in the worst of moments."

"What about you?" he asked. "What did this book mean for you?"

I was not used to being interviewed by Boškailo.

"For me it was about possibility," I said, "that survivors who had weathered what I thought of as unbearable pain could find joy again. They did not lose their view of the world as tragic or their sense of loss over not being the person they once were. But many found moments of happiness and a sense of purpose that transcended the tragedy. And you helped them get there by demonstrating that good and trusting relationships can exist."

Just as I had experienced secondary trauma, I was now reaping the benefits of secondary healing. I had listened to a story of tragedy until it had transformed into a story of possibility. This book is a testimony for me as well.

———

It is only fitting that our book should end in Bosnia. Boškailo needs Bosnia to recover if he and Aiša are ever to come back for more than a few weeks a year.

"I could not live in Bosnia and face my Croatian neighbors every day without asking them to explain their wartime activities," he told me. "I could not stand by while government agencies refused to hire Bosniaks."

But that does not mean he does not find joy on Bosnian soil. He and Aiša still like staying in the house Boškailo grew up in, sleeping on mattresses on the floor. Where else could they be with their extended family, the relatives who cook meals for them and stop by in the afternoon to give them fresh peaches from their gardens?

Boškailo still believes there is no healing without justice. He still wants to see Karadžić convicted in The Hague when the trial concludes.

But more important than a verdict, he says, is his ability to work again as a doctor and the support he receives from family and close friends.

Like Aiša, there are few activities he finds more enjoyable than driving to Sarajevo to walk along the cobblestone streets in the old city, just as they did before the war. A mosque, a synagogue, and a church share the same courtyard. During World War II, Muslims had hidden the Sarajevo Haggadah, an illuminated fourteenth-century manuscript that tells the story of the Exodus, and returned it to the Jewish community afterward. Boškailo's cousins had given me a beautiful bound copy of the illustrated Haggadah that I will always cherish.

During our visit to Bosnia, I walked one night in Sarajevo with the Boškailos. Hundreds of people wearing their best clothes—older women in long dresses and young girls in their tightest tops and shortest skirts—strolled past shops that sold clothing, candy, copper pots, and the like. Some nights, I was told, thousands stand shoulder to shoulder for the evening outing.

Aiša wore a flowing blue and red dress, and she and Boškailo walked arm in arm. They gathered cousins along the way, and the people they call their cousins, until they were a dozen strolling in unison.

"The goal of healing is to have some semblance of life before the trauma," Boškailo told me. "Before the war we were together. We are together again."

So we walked up and down the street, stopping for coffee at one café bar, walking some more, stopping for coffee at another café bar. It took ten minutes to move a few feet.

The beauty was in walking, slowly, without urgency, and the joy was contagious.

"I feel like I am a winner on these nights," Boškailo said, "like I'm shouting, 'I'm here again. Look at me. What you tried to do to me you couldn't.' I'm not half a person. I feel big. I feel important. I feel great. I can eat whenever I want. I can walk in any direction I want. I can have a cup of coffee anywhere I want."

They have a word for it in Bosnian, I remembered: *ćeif.* Extreme pleasure. Like life before the war.

Postscript

In May 2011, the sixty-nine-year-old Bosnian Serb commander Ratko Mladić was extradited to The Hague on charges of genocide. He had been commander of Bosnian Serb troops during the siege of Sarajevo and the mass killings at Srebrenica, and had been on the run for sixteen years.

In Belgrade, some ten thousand Serbian nationalists rallied against the arrest of a man they called a Serbian hero.

In his second court appearance in The Hague, the once-burly military leader looked frail and slurred his speech. He taunted the judges and broke into laughter. Then he pled for sympathy. He was "an elderly man and sickly," he said.

It was not the courtroom antics that moved Boškailo. It was the tears. According to his lawyer, Mladić cried during a farewell visit with his wife and sister. The man known as the Butcher of Bosnia was sobbing.

"It was a good feeling to hear he cried," Boškailo said. "And to know that he suffered for years in hiding, afraid every time he went out that somebody was going to get him. He must have felt like a trapped animal waiting to be killed."

Then, in late June, fifty-two-year-old Serbian Goran Hadžić was arrested for war crimes in Croatia, including the murder of hundreds of Croat and other non-Serb civilians by Croatian Serb troops.

Boškailo had shrugged off the death of Milošević. The capture of these last two fugitives was an unexpected victory.

"A few years back I was angrier, but I think I've changed in terms of my view of the court. The court made history, and the court determined what will be taught in the history books."

Twenty years ago the men in the camps had talked of Nuremberg. "The Hague should be Nuremberg for us," he said. "Some Bosnians feel we got too little too late. But today I know now that justice is never late."

Notes

We confirmed details of Boškailo's concentration camp experience with other camp survivors, including a leader of the Association of Concentration Camp Survivors of Bosnia-Herzegovina, as well as with documents produced by Human Rights Watch, Amnesty International, and the International Committee of the Red Cross.

Boškailo was a witness to much of the history we refer to in the notes. We have cited books, articles, and websites that also discuss these events.

Chapter 1
3   *epigraph*: Rumi, "The Story of My Life," trans. Nader Khalili, in *Rumi Fountain of Fire* (Hesperia, CA: Cal-Earth Press, 1994), 35.
5   *a psychiatrist worth listening to*: Gordon Allport, preface to Viktor Frankl, *Man's Search for Meaning* (New York: Simon and Schuster, 1984), 7.

Chapter 2
8   *epigraph*: Mak Dizdar, "Text about a Land," trans. Francis R. Jones, in *Scar on the Stone: Contemporary Poems from Bosnia*, ed. Chris Agee (Newcastle upon Tyne, UK: Bloodaxe Books, 1998), 29.

Chapter 3
13   *epigraph*: Abdulah Sidran, "Gavrilo," trans. Ted Hughes and Antonela Glavinić, in Agee, *Scar on the Stone*, 55.

Chapter 4
16   *epigraph*: Semezdin Mehmedinović, "An Essay," trans. Kathleen Jamie and Antonela Glavinić, in Agee, *Scar on the Stone*, 167.

16 *competing interpretations*: Sabrina Ramet, *Thinking about Yugoslavia: Scholarly Debates about the Yugoslav Breakup and the Wars in Bosnia and Kosovo* (Cambridge, UK: Cambridge University Press, 2005), ix, 3.

16 *lived peacefully*: Noel Malcolm, *Bosnia: A Short History* (New York: New York University Press, 1994), xxi.

16 *Archduke Franz Ferdinand*: Ibid., 155.

16 *Nazi Germany invaded*: Ibid., 174–75.

17 *the Ustasha executed*: Roy Gutman, *A Witness to Genocide* (New York: Macmillan, 1993), xxi.

17 *Foča-Čajniče region*: Malcolm, *Bosnia: A Short History*, 188.

17 *persuaded King Peter*: Ibid., 184.

17 *Tito liberated the region*: Marko Attila Hoare, *The History of Bosnia from the Middle Ages to the Present Day* (London: Saqi Books, 2007), 305–8.

17 *250,000 people were killed*: Malcolm, *Bosnia: A Short History*, 193.

17 *Tito began to liberalize*: Hoare, *History of Bosnia*, 324–28.

17 *Tito died*: Paul Mojzes, *Yugoslavian Inferno: Ethnoreligious Warfare in the Balkans* (New York: Continuum, 1994), 54–56.

18 *Slobodan Milošević came to power*: Tim Judah, "Death of Milošević: From Balkan Tyranny to a Lonely Cell," *Observer* (UK), March 12, 2006.

18 *controlled the well-equipped Yugoslav army*: Malcolm, *Bosnia: A Short History*, 243.

19 *Serbia attacked Croatia*: Hoare, *History of Bosnia*, 350.

19 *Bosnia as an independent state*: Ibid., 234.

19 *Karadžić . . . commanded a renegade Serbian army*: International Criminal Tribunal for the Former Yugoslavia, "Case Information Sheet (IT-95-5/18): Radovan Karadžić," *www.icty.org/x/cases/karadzic/cis/en/cis_karadzic_en.pdf*.

19 *ethnic cleansing*: Malcolm, *Bosnia: A Short History*, 246.

19 *a Greater Serbia*: Ibid., 229, 246.

19 *United Nations sent peacekeepers*: Hoare, *History of Bosnia*, 377.

20 *Serb conquerors . . . have established two concentration camps*: Gutman, *Witness to Genocide*, 44.

20 *a natural alliance*: Hoare, *History of Bosnia*, 366–69.

27 *Animosity between Croats and Bosniaks*: Malcolm, *Bosnia: A Short History*, 232–33.

Chapter 5

29 *epigraph*: Excerpt from "Wedding" is taken from page 65 of *Mak Dizdar: Stone Sleeper*, translated by Francis R. Jones, published by Anvil Press Poetry (London), 2009.

30 *Strange suffering*: Unpublished translation by Mirza Bašić.

30 *Germans and Italians had invaded*: Malcolm, *Bosnia: A Short History*, 173.

31 *war broke out between the Croats and the Bosniaks*: Ibid., 248–49.

37 *Water ran*: Lyrics from the website *World of Sevdah*, "Mejra na tabutu," trans. Mirza Bašić, January 27, 2009, *worldofsevdah.com/ mejra-na-tabutu/.

Chapter 6

38 *epigraph*: Mak Dizdar, "Blue River," trans. Francis R. Jones, in Agee, *Scar on the Stone*, 6.

42 *Mother was waking up Sejdefa*: Lyrics from the website *World of Sevdah*, "Sejdefu majka budila," trans. Mirza Bašić, September 19, 2009, *worldofsevdah.com/sejdefu-majka-budila/*.

46 *Šurmanci*: Richard West, "'Convert a Third, Kill a Third,'" *Guardian*, August 20, 1992.

Chapter 7

47 *epigraphs*: Rumi, "On the Deathbed," *www.rumi.org.uk/ poems.html*; Ilija Ladin, "A Stone Wedding," trans. Ken Smith and Igor Klikovac, in Agee, *Scar on the Stone*, 99.

49 *My Bosnia, beautiful country*: "My Bosnia, Beautiful Country," trans. Esad Boškailo.

57 *fifteen thousand Bosnian Muslims*: UN High Commissioner for Refugees, cited in Human Rights Watch, "Abuses by Bosnian Croat and Muslim Forces in Central and Southwestern Bosnia-Hercegovina," September 1993, 4.

57 *twenty-four detention centers*: International Committee of the Red Cross, cited in Amnesty International, "Bosnia-Herzegovina: Deliberate and Arbitrary Detentions of Civilians / Fear of Torture, Ill-Treatment and Deliberate and Arbitrary Killings: Detained Croatian and Serbian Civilians and Captured Combatants in Bosnia-Herzegovina," Document UA 318/93, September 1993, 1.

57 *ill-treatment and inhuman conditions*: Ibid.

58 *delegates of the International Committee of the Red Cross*: International Committee of the Red Cross, cited in Amnesty International, "Bosnia-Herzegovina: Deliberate and Arbitrary

Detention of Civilians / Deliberate and Arbitrary Killings / Fear of Torture and Ill-Treatment: Detained Muslim Civilians and Prisoners of War in Bosnian Croat Controlled Areas of Bosnia-Herzegovina," Document UA 315/93, September 1993, 1–2.

58 *allowed access to Dretelj*: Ibid., 1.
58 *A British journalist reported*: Ibid., 2.
58 *Representatives of the UN High Commissioner for Refugees*: Cited in ibid., 2.
58 *Those released complained*: Chuck Sudetic, "Released Muslim Prisoners Report Abuses at Bosnian Croatian Camps," *New York Times*, September 7, 1993.
58 *reporter Ed Vulliamy*: Ed Vulliamy, "Concentration Camps," in *Crimes of War*, ed. Roy Gutman and David Rieff (New York: Norton, 1999), 105–6.

Chapter 8
59 *epigraph*: Abdulah Sidran, "Gavrilo," trans. Ted Hughes and Antonela Glavinić, in Agee, *Scar on the Stone*, 55.
60 *"Blue River"*: Mak Dizdar, "Blue River," trans. Francis R. Jones, in Agee, *Scar on the Stone*, 6.

Chapter 9
72 *epigraph*: Excerpt from "BBBB" is taken from page 54 of *Mak Dizdar: Stone Sleeper*, translated by Francis R. Jones, published by Anvil Press Poetry (London), 2009.
73 *July 1995*: Hoare, History of Bosnia, 393.
73 *killed more than eight thousand*: Ibid., 393.
73 *expelled some twenty thousand*: Gregory Katz, "Serbs Mount New Attack on Muslims; Europeans Consider Call for Action," *Dallas Morning News*, July 15, 1995.
73 *air strikes*: Deutsche Presse-Agentur, "NATO Launches Unprecedented Air Campaign against Bosnian Serbs," August 30, 1995.
74 *the playwright Harold Pinter and the former U.S. attorney general Ramsey Clark*: Petition of the International Committee to Defend Slobodan Milošević, signed by Harold Pinter, Ramsey Clark, and others, at the website of *The Emperor's New Clothes*, emperor.vwh.net/petition/petition.htm.
74 *Dayton Peace Accords*: Hoare, *History of Bosnia*, 398–99.
74 *200,000 dead*: Almir Arnaut, "U.S. Troops Mark End of Mission in Bosnia," Associated Press, November 24, 2004.

74 *2.7 million refugees*: John Roberts and Angeline Oyog, "Bosnia-Herzegovina Refugees: Displaced Are the Real Losers of War," IPS (Inter Press Service), December 6, 1995.

Chapter 10

79 *epigraph*: Excerpt from "Roads" is taken from page 17 of *Mak Dizdar: Stone Sleeper*, translated by Francis R. Jones, published by Anvil Press Poetry (London), 2009.

79 *clung to his image of Aiša*: Frankl, *Man's Search for Meaning*, 49–52.

79 *multitude of small torments*: Ibid., 17.

79 *grown men huddling*: Ibid., 30.

79 *capos*: Ibid., 18–19.

79 *small miracles*: Ibid., 30.

80 *edema*: Ibid., 39.

80 *apathy*: Ibid., 33, 71.

80 *best of us did not return*: Ibid., 19.

80 *attitude toward the suffering*: Ibid., 148.

80 *being questioned by life*: Ibid., 85.

80 *right action*: Ibid., 74.

80 *meaning through suffering*: Ibid., 86.

81 *three different ways*: Ibid., 115, 146.

Chapter 11

85 *epigraph*: Excerpt from "Madderfield" is taken from page 61 of *Mak Dizdar: Stone Sleeper*, translated by Francis R. Jones, published by Anvil Press Poetry (London), 2009.

87 *hierarchies of suffering*: Jonathan Shay, *Achilles in Vietnam: Combat Trauma and the Undoing of Character* (New York: Simon and Schuster, 1995), 192.

Chapter 12

88 *epigraph*: Abdulah Sidran, "Chronicle of a Miracle," trans. Ted Hughes and Antonela Glavinić, in Agee, *Scar on the Stone*, 65.

88 *If anyone needed soothing*: Pseudonyms have been used in place of patients' real names.

91 *biological miracle of empathy*: Richard F. Mollica, *Healing Invisible Wounds: Paths to Hope and Recovery in a Violent World* (New York: Harcourt, 2006), 97, 115.

91 *quality of the relationship*: Viktor Frankl, *The Will to Meaning*:

Foundations and Applications of Logotherapy (New York: Penguin, 1988), 6, 8.

92 *defined by the American Psychiatric Association*: American Psychiatric Association (APA), "Post-Traumatic Stress Disorder," *Diagnostic and Statistical Manual of Mental Disorders*, 4th ed. (Washington, DC: APA, 2000).

92 *suffering from "nostalgia"*: Anthony Babington, *Shell-Shock: A History of the Changing Attitudes to War Neurosis* (London: Leo Cooper, 1997), 8, 46, 151.

92 *Survivors of the Holocaust*: Paul Chodoff, "Psychotherapy of the Survivor," in *Survivors, Victims, and Perpetrators: Essays on the Nazi Holocaust*, ed. Joel Dimsdale (New York: Hemisphere, 1980), 205–6.

92 *Classic symptoms of PTSD*: APA, "Post-Traumatic Stress Disorder."

92 *first text on the treatment of PTSD*: Frank Ochberg, *Post-Traumatic Therapy and Victims of Violence* (New York: Brunner/Mazel, 1988).

93 *an event of major dimension*: Frank Ochberg, "PTSD 101," Dart Center for Journalism and Trauma, *dartcenter.org/content/ptsd-101-0*.

93 *prevalence of PTSD*: Edna B. Foa et al., *Effective Treatments for PTSD: Practice Guidelines from the International Society for Traumatic Stress Studies* (New York: Guilford Press, 2009), 6.

93 *The higher incidence among women*: Foa et al., *Effective Treatments for PTSD*, 6.; David F. Tolin and Edna B. Foa, "Sex Differences in Trauma and Posttraumatic Stress Disorder: A Quantitative Review of 25 Years of Research," *Psychological Bulletin* 132, no. 6 (2006): 981.

93 *returning troops from Iraq and Afghanistan*: Terri Tanielian and Lisa H. Joycox, eds., *Invisible Wounds of War: Psychological and Cognitive Injuries, Their Consequences and Services to Assist Recovery* (Santa Monica, CA: Rand Center for Military Health Policy Research, 2008), 3.

93 *The results of controlled trials*: Foa et al., *Effective Treatments for PTSD*, 98.

93 *Some professionals reject*: Chris R. Brewin, *Post-Traumatic Stress Disorder: Malady or Myth?* (New Haven, CT: Yale University Press, 2003), 1–2, 31, 33.

94 *extensively investigated and well-validated disorder*: Foa et al., *Effective Treatments for PTSD*, 24.

94 *cognitive therapy is effective*: Ibid., 198–99.

94 *Another method shown to be valuable*: Ibid., 298.

95 *power of storytelling*: Mollica, *Healing Invisible Wounds*, 115.

95 *the psychologist Jack Saul*: Rob Waters, "Surviving Disaster," *Psychotherapy Networker* 28, no. 4 (2004): 40–41.

Chapter 13

101 *epigraph*: Abdulah Sidran, "Sarajevo Sings," trans. Ted Hughes and Antonela Glavinić, in Agee, *Scar on the Stone*, 66.

104 *professional neutrality*: Robert Jay Lifton, *The Future of Immortality* (New York: HarperCollins, 1988), 243.

104 *morally engaged*: Shay, *Achilles in Vietnam*, 194.

105 *morally impossible to remain neutral*: Judith Herman, *Trauma and Recovery* (New York: Basic Books, 1997), 7.

107 *God's love for humankind*: Shay, *Achilles in Vietnam*, 148.

107 *Boškailo agreed with Victor Frankl*: Frankl, *The Will to Meaning*, 145.

108 *forgive on behalf of the dead*: Elie Wiesel, *Messengers of God: Biblical Portraits and Legends* (New York: Simon & Schuster, 1985), 234.

109 *Frankl's logotherapy*: Frankl, *Man's Search for Meaning*, 104.

110 *symbolic immortality*: Robert Jay Lifton, *The Protean Self* (Chicago: University of Chicago Press, 1999), 29.

110 *survivor mission*: Herman, *Trauma and Recovery*, 207–11.

110 *deeper meaning to his life*: Frankl, *Man's Search for Meaning*, 76.

110 *transcriptions of his conversations*: Frankl, *The Will to Meaning*, 126–31.

Chapter 14

113 *epigraph*: Abdulah Sidran, "Those Who Cross," trans. Ted Hughes and Antonela Glavinić, in Agee, *Scar on the Stone*, 61

113 *killed eight thousand civilians*: Almir Arnaut, "Bosnia: Families Bury 308 Srebrenica Victims on 13th Anniversary of the Massacre," Associated Press, July 11, 2008.

113 *More than five thousand people*: Kara Sundby, "Times Topics: Srebrenica Massacre," *New York Times*, August 3, 2010.

113 *Some three thousand*: Arnaut, "Bosnia: Families Bury 308 Srebrenica Victims."

114 *an "inoculation"*: Ochberg, "PTSD 101."

114 *Gulf War veterans*: Foa et al., *Effective Treatments for PTSD*, 5.

116 *abnormal situation*: Frankl, *Man's Search for Meaning*, 32.

118 *not-so-mysterious force*: Mollica, *Healing Invisible Wounds*, 4.

120 *tragic optimism*: Frankl, *Man's Search for Meaning*, 139.

120 *how to celebrate*: Judith Lewis Herman, *Trauma and Recovery* (New York: Basic Books, 1997), 213.

Chapter 15

122 *epigraph*: Excerpt from "A Text about a Spring" is taken from page 35 of *Mak Dizdar: Stone Sleeper*, translated by Francis R. Jones, published by Anvil Press Poetry (London), 2009.

124 *reveal their own experiences with trauma*: Andrei Novac, "Special Considerations in the Treatment of Traumatized Patients," *Psychiatric Times* 19, no. 2 (2002): 92–93.

127 *illuminating in its pain*: Lifton, *The Protean Self*, 82.

127 *recovery is based*: Herman, *Trauma and Recovery*, 211.

Chapter 16

128 *epigraph*: Radovan Karadžić, "Let's Go Down to the Town and Kill Some Scum," quoted in Mark Danner, "Bosnia: The Turning Point," *New York Review of Books*, February 5, 1998.

128 *the Bosnian Serb leader charged with genocide*: International Criminal Tribunal for the Former Yugoslavia, "Statement of the Office of the Prosecutor on the Arrest of Radovan Karadžić," July 21, 2008.

129 *New Age natural healer*: Jack Hitt, "Radovan Karadžić's New-Age Adventure," *New York Times*, July 26, 2009.

129 *Milošević had died*: Marlise Simons and Alison Smale, "Slobodan Milošević, 64, Former Yugoslav Leader Accused of War Crimes, Dies," *New York Times*, March 12, 2006.

130 *opening statement*: Ian Traynor, "War Crimes Tribunal: 'A Just and Holy Cause,'" *Guardian*, March 2, 2010.

130 *Milan Mandilović*: International Criminal Tribunal for the Former Yugoslavia, "Transcript of Court Proceedings, July 19, 2010," 5414.

131 *Hussein Ali Abdel-Razec*: Ibid., 5513–16.

134 *witnesses in The Hague*: Eric Stover, *The Witnesses: War Crimes and the Promise of Justice in the Hague* (Philadelphia: University of Pennsylvania Press, 2005), 103, 129, 132–33.

135 *Karadžić's lawyer-adviser*: Peter Robinson, "Defending the Damned: The Role of Defense Counsel in International Criminal Cases," speech delivered at Oxford University, February 22, 2010. A podcast of Robinson's speech is available at *www.peterrobinson.com*.

136 *Pinter*: Petition of the International Committee to Defend

Slobodan Milošević, signed by Pinter and others, at the website of *The Emperor's New Clothes, emperor.vwh.net/petition/petition.htm.*

136 *Solzhenitsyn*: Greg Myre, "War in the Balkans: Protest," *Independent*, April 29, 1999.

136 *Chomsky had signed*: Letter reprinted by the *Nordic News Network* in Al Burke, "All Quieted on the Word Front" (2005), 31, *www.nnn.se/n-model/foreign/ordfront.pdf.*

136 *the hypothesis can at least be advanced*: Diana Johnstone, *Fools' Crusade: Yugoslavia, NATO and Western Delusions* (New York: Monthly Review Press, 2002), 109.

136 *a brutal little civil war*: Ibid., 53.

136 *greatly exaggerated*: Ibid., 79.

136 *journalists had been duped*: Ibid., 76.

136 *Vulliamy . . . accused Chomsky*: Ed Vulliamy, "Open Letter to Amnesty International," October 31, 2009, from the website of the Congress of North American Bosniaks, *www.bosniak.org/ open-letter-from-ed-vulliamy-to-amnesty-international/.*

137 *brutal and inhumane actions*: APA, "Resolution Condemning the Role of Psychiatrist Radovan Karadžić in Human Rights Abuses in the Former Yugoslavia," March 1993, *www.psych.org/Departments/EDU/ Library/APAOfficialDocumentsandRelated/PositionStatements/199301. aspx.*

137 *imprisoned only briefly*: David Charter, "Serb Fugitive Will Face Genocide Charges," *Times* (London), July 22, 2008.

137 *never distinguished himself as a doctor*: "The World's Most Wanted Man," *Frontline*, PBS, prod. Pippa Scott, May 26, 1998.

137 *Jovan Rašković*: United Press International, "Krajina Serbs Announce Challenge to Rebel Leader," February 4, 1992.

137 *concept of "doubling"*: Robert Jay Lifton, *The Nazi Doctors* (New York: Basic Books, 1986), 417–33.

138 *Nazi Max de Crinis*: Ibid., 120–23.

138 *biological romanticism*: Ibid., 40.

Chapter 17

139 *epigraphs*: Excerpt from "A Text about a Knight" is taken from page 78 of *Mak Dizdar: Stone Sleeper*, translated by Francis R. Jones, published by Anvil Press Poetry (London), 2009; Fahrudin Zilkić, "The Last Men," trans. Francis R. Jones, in Agee, *Scar on the Stone*, 200.

139 *Three thousand victims*: Arnaut, "Bosnia: Families Bury 308
Srebrenica Victims."
140 *fleeing toward Tuzla*: Ibid.
140 *safe place*: James Bolin and Tim Judah, "UN to Enforce No-Fly
Zone as Aid Reaches Srebrenica, *Times*, March 20, 1993.
140 *Serb troops led by General Ratko Mladić*: Arnaut, "Bosnia: Families
Bury 308 Srebrenica Victims."
141 *Annan called it one of the darkest days*: Daniel McLaughlin,
"Mourners Finally Get to Bury Their Loved Ones," *Irish Times*,
July 12, 2005.
141 *Bosnian president Haris Silajdžić*: "Bosnia Marks 13th Anniversary
of Genocide," *Bosnia News*, July 11, 2008.
141 *U.S. ambassador*: "Remarks by H. E. English Charles, U.S. Ambassador
to Bosnia and Herzegovina," U.S. Department of State, July 11, 2008.
141 *Mustafa Cerić*: "Bosnia Marks 13th Anniversary of Genocide,"
Bosnia News.
141 *Sabaheta Fejzić*: "13th Anniversary of Srebrenica Genocide," *Srebrenica
Genocide Blog, srebrenica-genocide.blogspot.com/*, July 14, 2008.
141 *Dutch soldier*: Ibid.

Chapter 18
143 *epigraphs*: Izet Sarajlić, "Untitled," trans. Charles Simić, in
Agee, *Scar on the Stone*, 70; Izet Sarajlić, "Softly with a Touch of
Sadness," trans. Charles Simić, in Agee, *Scar on the Stone*, 72.
144 *Dayton Peace Accords*: Elaine Sciolino, "Balkan Accord:
The Overview; Accord Reached to End the War in Bosnia;
Clinton Pledges U.S. Troops to Keep Peace," *New York Times*,
November 22, 1995.

Chapter 19
152 *epigraphs*: Semezdin Mehmedinović, "An Essay," trans. Kathleen
James, in Agee, *Scar on the Stone*, 167; Ranko Sladojević, "Saturday
Idyll," trans. Harry Clifton, in Agee, *Scar on the Stone*, 124.
152 *three acts in the news coverage*: Frank Ochberg, "Trauma News:
Stories in Three Acts," *Gift from Within: PTSD Resources for
Survivors and Caregivers*, February 22, 1999, *www.giftfromwithin
.org/html/threeact.html*.

Postscript

157 *Mladić was extradited*: International Criminal Tribunal for the Former Yugoslavia, "Tribunal Welcomes the Arrest of Ratko Mladić," May 26, 2011.

157 *Serbian nationalists rallied*: Steven Erlanger, "Demonstrators Rally against Mladić Extradition," *New York Times*, May 29, 2011.

157 *In his second court appearance*: Marlise Simons, "Hague Judge Orders Mladić Removed from Courtroom," *New York Times*, July 4, 2011.

157 *Mladić cried*: Dragana Jovanović, "Bosnian Serb Ex-Military Commander Headed to the Hague," *ABC News*, May 31, 2011.

157 *Hadžić was arrested*: International Criminal Tribunal for the Former Yugoslavia, "Tribunal Welcomes the Arrest of Goran Hadžić," July 20, 2011.

Index